First Step Act-
Pre-Release Earned Time Credit Programs & Activities: Bureau of Prisons Efforts to Undermine Incentive Programming, 2019-2022

Federal Sentencing Alliance
Ralph S. Behr

© 2021

TABLE OF CONTENTS-

Introduction viii

PART 1

More Introductory Information:

Programs "Utilization" & "Implementation" Delays 1

How Disparities And Failures Started 2

Time Credit "Awarded" Disparities 6

The *Proverbial* Writing On The Wall 7

Time Credit "Application" Failures 10

Matters Of First Impression 14

The COVID-19 Pandemic 15

Relay Race With A Rocky Start 17

Not A Neutral Playing Field 19

TABLE OF CONTENTS-
PART II.

First Step Act of 2018: Risk and Needs Assessment System - Incentive Programming Implementation Delays, Disparities & Failures	
Introduction	21
Initial PATTERN Tool (Prototype)	27
Mandatory Authority Granted To The Bureau Of Prisons To Use Then Existing Incentive Programming	30
BOP Ignored the Act's Mandate For Immediate Utilization of Earned Time Credit Incentives, Pursuant To 18 U.S.C.§§ 3621(h)(4)(6)(2019)	39
In Section 102, Subsection (4), First Step Act "May" Means "Must" Welcome to Congressional Semantics	40
Hypothetical Use Of Semantics	41
Section 102(4) of the First Step Act Of 2018, and 18 U.S.C. § 3621(h)(4),	

TABLE OF CONTENTS-

Word "May" Really Means "Must", as "May" Merely Grants Authority To BOP To Utilize Previously Existing Programs And Activities	45
The Word "May"	45
The Word "System"	48
The Word "Implementation" Or "Implement" And Its Usage In The Act	52
The First Step Act Of 2018, Sec. 102 (4)	56
The First Step Act Of 2018, Sec. 102 (6)	56
Senator Richard Durbin and Senator Chuck Grassley, Letter to Attorney General Merrick Garland, May 5, 2021 Regarding First Step Act Earned Time Credits Disparities and Failures	57
November 25, 2020 Bureau of Prisons published Earned Time Credit (Proposed Rules) in the Federal Register	67

TABLE OF CONTENTS-

PART III.

DOJ /BOP Early Release Time Credit Incentives Programming Implementation and Planned Time Credit Awards Planned for Pre-release Custody Determination *in Para Flagrante Delicto*, Violates the First Step Act and Effectively Renders 18 U.S.C. § 3632(d)(4)(2020) *Ultra Vires*

Introduction	73
The Operative Statute- 18 U.S.C. § 3632(d)(4)(2020)	76
Four Year College Degree Hypothetical- A Literal Reading Of 18 U.S.C. § 3632 (d)(4) (2020) Would Lead to this Result	78
DOJ/BOP Reading Of 18 U.S.C. § 3632 (d)(4)(2019)	80
The AG Barr Fallacy *Sounding In Semantics*: This was the AG Barr Reading of the Law using Semantics	83

TABLE OF CONTENTS-

The Approved And Vetted List Of Programs And Planned Application Of Credits	85
The Inmate English Student Productive Activity Example Cited From "The List"	86
What AG Barr has *subtly done* here is the following	89
18 U.S.C. § 3621(h)(6)(2020), Section 102 First Step Act Of 2018	92
Remedies/BOP Time Credit Anomaly Issues	93
No BOP Rule Federal Register Press	94

TABLE OF CONTENTS-

PART IV.

First Step Act Early Release Time Credits Earned in 2020-2021 May Not Be Timely Applied to an Inmate's Time Credit Account until on or after January 22, 2022

More Semantics: Permissive Authority verses Mandatory Authority Arguments Made	100
A Word About Bureau of Prison Policy	102
What Is The Genus Of The Bureau Of Prisons Argument For The January 20, 2022 To Be "Applied" Drop Dead Date?	104
The Minority U.S. District Court Opinion (*Goodman v. Ortiz*)	108
The *Goodman* Court's Conclusion	111
The *Goodman* Case Rollout	115

TABLE OF CONTENTS-

The Majority View	116
Cumulative Effect of Implementation Disparities, Time Credit Award Disparities, and Time Credit Application Failures, and Current Efforts To Fix The Broken System	130
The Term *Trojan Horse*	132
The 2021-2022 117th Congressional Session	133
COVID–19 Safer Detention Act of 2021	135
First Step Implementation Act 2021	137
Critical Thinking	140
About Author Federal Sentencing Alliance	141
About Author Ralph S. Behr	144

INTRODUCTION

Former Attorney General William Barr's administration, over a two year period, effectively skinned, gutted and killed what Congress enacted in The First Step Act regarding pre-release time credit incentive programming. With every policy, with every guideline, and with every rule promulgated, Congress' Act was either ignored, undermined or overruled by Barr's administration. At the present time what remains is a sarcophagus of First Step Act incentive programming. This must end. The new administration should Do-Over and fix the damage done by Attorney General Barr's administration during the period 2019-2020, that remains in place today.

Read this book and speak out. The 2021-2022

117th Congress needs to fix legislative "loopholes" in that permitted Barr to undermine and corrupt the intended beneficial effects of pre-release incentive programming in a short time. Barr achieved this undermining by ignoring Congressional Act mandates, by creating unauthorized time delays, through manipulation of procedures, by promulgating adverse implementation and application rules, and by adopting adverse policies, contrary to the Act.

Here is the short list of what is broken and why:

- The Attorney General's Office never released a complete Needs and Assessment System on July 19, 2019, but rather, only released a prototype PATTERN tool on that date, called a complete system. *See* 18 U.S.C. § 3632(a)(2019).

- The needs component of the Needs and Assessment System was not released until January 20, 2020, 6 months late, that was the approved and vetted (6 page) listing of recidivism reduction programs and productive activities ("List"). The List was one month late, per page. *Id.*
- Immediately after the First Step Act was enacted on December 21, 2018, the Bureau of Prisons had mandatory authority, pursuant to 18 U.S.C. § 3632(a)(2019), to use "then existing" risk and needs assessment tools available, to permit inmates to engage in "then existing" recidivism reduction programs and productive activities for earned time credits during the preliminary phase in period, pursuant to 18 U.S.C. § 3621(h)(4) (2019). Inmates certainly engaged recidivism

reduction programs and productive activities in 2019, but have yet to get time credits <u>voluntarily</u> applied by the Bureau of Prisons for 2019 incentive programming, The Bureau of Prisons does not want to award 2019 time credits. What happened to the time credits earned from December 21, 2018 through January 19, 2020 one might ask? Why aren't they applied?

- Now a recent Bureau of Prisons "Rule", that was published in the Federal Register on November 25, 2020, states that the Bureau of Prisons will not award ANY First Step Act pre-release earned time credits for recidivism reduction programs or productive activities successfully completed, prior to January 20, 2020.
- The List released on January 20, 2020 purports to authorize the "award" of a stated number of

"hours" (in class time only), that in no way comports with days of program or activity participation contemplated by the First Step Act. The hours awarded, cited within the four corners of the List, is absurd; rendering it impossible for anybody to meaningfully earn pre-release time credits, for 'hours' cited in the List.

- Earned Time Credits inmates deserve from December 21, 2018 through January 20, 2020, should, must and will be granted if we speak out to our Congressional Leadership.

- The new operative Bureau Of Prisons policy is that time credits can be earned, based on successful completion of a program or activity, but that the Bureau of Prisons is not mandated to timely apply those earned time credits to benefit the inmate who earned them.

Where did that landmine come from? And why?

- The Bureau of Prisons has managed to convince a majority of District Court Judges reviewing the untimely "applied credits" issue, that it is not mandated to apply awarded time credits to an inmates time card until on or after January 20, 2022. <u>That's right January 20, 2022.</u> What about all the inmates that were already, or will be released time served in 2019-2021? That means that thousands of inmates may not receive the benefit of any earned time credits whatsoever.

- Thereafter, considering that the Bureau of Prisons is (presently) not mandated to apply time credits earned until after January 20, 2022, who is to say that the Bureau of Prisons won't just make a new Rule that they are not going to apply time credits earned prior to

January 20, 2022? Sounds far fetched? Maybe, but maybe not, considering the way that inmate's rights regarding time credits have been skeletonized.

- Since December 21, 2018 the Bureau of Prisons actually corrupted the Act, through the use of 'word meaning' semantics, and constructively corrupted the Act, through wilful ignorance of core Act provisions, mandates and time periods [hereinafter "shenanigans"].

- Here is a laundry list of activities by the Bureau of Prisons intended to keep confidential, for as long as possible, real operational policies, procedures, and plans, regarding pre-release time credit incentive programming matters, at any given moment in time:

> -Officially stated policies and/or procedures on the BOP Website change to latent unofficial policies and/or procedures without notice;

-Stated policies are different than actual unofficial policies in use, at any given moment in time;

-Unofficial policies and/or procedures change without notice, because they do not officially exist;

-Important Federal Register Rule changes do not appear on the Bureau of Prisons Website timely, or at all; and

-Unofficial (confidential) policies of the Bureau of Prisons are oftentimes stated in Court for the first time, as official policy, when they are not official policy.

o In so doing, the Bureau of Prisons corrupted the Act and achieved these things, contrary to the Act:

-Erosion of inmates' substantive First Step Act rights through Rule promulgation;

-Word semantics, ignoring Congressional intent;

-Unauthorized latent implementation time delays;

-Undermining incentive programming incentive;

-Ignoring Congressional mandates, as though they were never written;

-Unfair practices regarding Rule promulgation;

-Capitalizing on inmates' lack of Court standing;

-Fundamental unfairness to inmates without adequate remedy at law;

-Violation of substantial fairness and good faith; and

-Other arbitrary, capricious, and self serving actions taken, eviscerating inmates' rights to timely application of time credits earned.

The Authors do not take these allegations lightly.

The Authors believe that all of the disparities and failures delineated in this publication, as achieved by the Attorney General William Barr administration, together with then Bureau of Prisons' policy and procedure makers in calendar years 2019-2020, are opposites to the spirit and intent of the First Step Act.

The System is broken, but can be fixed in the short term with immediate support received from new Attorney General Merrick Garland, Senator Dick Durbin (D-IL), primary author of the First Step Act of 2018, and the 2021-2022 117th Congress.

Federal Sentencing Alliance has been, and will remain, on top of these issues as they develop, with an eye toward identification of additional First Step Act loopholes, and recommendation for legislative patches.

PART 1

MORE INTRODUCTORY INFORMATION-

Programs "Utilization" & "Implementation" Delays-

Although the First Step Act incentive programming U.S. Code provisions create substantive rights for inmate rights, the Act does not provide standing, *per se,* for an inmate to complain to a District Court Judge to seek redress for time credit disparities or failures, however, many inmates have done so anyway, using other legal theories conferring subject matter jurisdiction to a District Court.

In order to fix a broken system it is necessary to first identify what is broken with enough detail to see how it got broken. That is why this book was written: To identify, with specificity, what is broken in order to facilitate actual redress by inmates seeking to meaningfully embrace and benefit from earned time credit substantive provisions of the First Step Act.

That includes from December 21, 2018 through the date of this publication, and going forward into 2022.

How Disparities And Failures Started-

The Bureau of Prisons missed mandatory "utilization" (of previously existing programs and activities, during the preliminary phase in period of 2019) and mandatory "implementation" due dates under the First Step Act Of 2018, Risk And Needs Assessment System in 2019, causing front end delays throughout calendar years 2019-2020, only to become further delayed by the COVID-19 Pandemic.

All missed mandatory due dates are examined in this publication, together with statutory citations and relevant caselaw for the issues presented.

The Authors believe that Congress intended early release time credit programming incentives to be immediately effective on and after December 21, 2018, and that the Bureau of Prisons was mandated by Congress to utilize then existing programs and activities in each respective facility, to immediately engage inmates in incentive programming during the phase in period, mostly comprising calendar year 2019.

Federal inmates did indeed complete recidivism reduction programs and productive activities in 2019, but have been unable to get time credits applied for successful completion; presumably because the approved and vetted List was officially published on January 20, 2020. It appears that the Bureau of Prisons simply ignored the Congressional mandate to utilize existing programs and activities for incentive programming purposes under the Act.

Now, the Bureau of Prisons has stated that an inmate cannot be awarded early release time credits for programs and activities completed prior to January 20, 2020. What happened to December 22, 2018 through January 19, 2020, also authorized by the First Step Act? A 6 month List release delay is circular to this issue.

January 20, 2020, was the date that Attorney General Barr released the vetted and approved programs and activities listing (6 months overdue) in an online published document titled *Evidence-based Recidivism*

Reduction (EBRR) Programs and Productive Activities (PA). So, right off the bat, inmates lost 13 months of incentive time credit programming, mandated by the First Step Act. To date, the Bureau of Prisons has refused to <u>voluntarily</u> recognize inmate time credits earned in 2019 under the First Step Act. It may take Court intervention to force changes that are much needed now.

These anomalies have created disparities that continue to this day, as most federal inmates nationwide were eager, qualified, and able, to embrace early release time credit incentive programming in 2019-2020, but many were not afforded that opportunity. These disparities are spawned from actual benefits provided by the Act, without meaningful remedies provided by law, for inmates to actually or fully realize the benefits created by the Act, to the maximum extent possible.

Qualified inmates have statutory rights to engage time credit programming and activities for the entire length of their incarcerative sentences, post December 21, 2018. Yet, many inmates will be released from custody prior to January 20, 2022, without realizing any earned time credit benefits under the Act, due to *latent* implementation delays, reduced actual time credit awards, and complete failures of the Bureau of Prisons to timely apply credits earned to inmate time credit accounts in a timely manner.

Time Credit "Awarded" Disparities-

Earned time credits do not reduce an inmate's sentence, but rather, are intended to be used by the BOP as a means to permit certain inmates to be transferred from their Bureau of Prisons incarcerative sentence to home confinement, to a community center, or to another halfway house type pre-release custody.

The idea is that when an inmates earned time credits are equal to the balance of that person's incarcerative sentence remaining, that the inmate will be extricated from the Bureau of Prisons, while still being monitored under the watchful eye of the Bureau. 18 U.S.C. § 3624(g)(2019). It is axiomatic that the less time credits that get applied will result in a longer incarcerative sentence. That is the BOP's motive here.

The *Proverbial* Writing On The Wall-

On January 20, 2020, the Bureau Of Prisons finally released the Attorney General's highly anticipated *approved and vetted* list of Evidence-based Recidivism Reduction Programs and Productive Activities (e.g. "*The List*" or "List"), as found here: https://www.bop.gov/inmates/fsa/docs/evidence_based_recidivism_reduction_programs.pdf

The List was released six months late, without any penalty, notice, or public outcry. Detailed reasons why *The List* was released 6 months late are detailed in this publication.

Analysis of *The List* reveals that the awarded time credits will be markedly lower than inmates expect to received from a plain reading of the First Step Act. Hours awarded on the List appear markedly lower, because they are markedly lower. The Bureau of Prisons, based on its interpretation of related First Step Act provisions awarding time credits, has decided to award "hours" instead of complete days for participation in incentive programming. The Act was intended to award time credits based upon days of program participation, not based upon how many actual hours are spent sitting in the classroom. The result of the Bureau of Prisons policy regarding minuscule time credit awards, hours not days, means that many inmates <u>cannot</u> meaningfully reduce the incarcerative portion of their sentences, prior to being released time served anyway.

Time credit "award" disparities appear within the four corners of *The List* itself, published on January 20, 2020. Again, there was no public notice, outcry, or press.

For instance, one of the vetted and approved programs is titled Resolve Program (Trauma Treatment) that is an 80 hour class over 40 weeks. The Bureau of Prisons intends to award 80 hours for successful completion. In that one example, the inmate will have served 10 months in prison and will be awarded 26.67 hours of time credits (80/3), assuming one prior minimal to low PATTERN risk assessment. If the Bureau of Prisons computes one day to mean an 8 hour day, that will amount to 3 days of time credits for successful completion of a 280 day class. You get the idea. In order to earn a year of time credits under that methodology one would need to be incarcerated for decades.

    The Authors have set forth all of the specific details regarding pre-release time credit application disparities and failures below, resulting from broad use of *application semantics* not intended by Congress.

Time Credit "Application" Failures-

This is a complete failure of the system that first came to light in mid-2020 that continues to this day. The Bureau of Prisons has argued at the District Court level that it is not mandated to apply earned time credits to inmate's time accounts until on or after January 20, 2022. The Authors see no justifiable basis for this arbitrary and capricious delayed application date. This utter failure violates the immediacy spirit of the First Step Act and the intent of Congress in passing the Act.

Since the First Step Act never specifically conferred standing for an inmate to complain directly to a federal judge regarding early release earned time credit disparities, the Bureau of Prisons has sadly taken advantage of that fact. The new tact being fostered by the Bureau of Prisons is that it is not mandated to apply time credits already earned by inmates, until on or after January 22, 2022. What that means is that it can if it wants to, but doesn't have to, timely apply earned time credits to any inmates time credit account.

There should be uniformity and transparency regarding Bureau of Prisons policies and procedures. Otherwise there is no accountability whatsoever. All too often however, nobody knows what a new policy is on any given issue, until the Bureau of Prisons announces it in Court for the first time. All too often however, District Courts buy into conclusions of law stated by the Bureau of Prisons, without even asking the Bureau of Prisons to cite legal justification or authority for their stated policy or Rule. The BOP's policies must be in alignment.

A natural issue arises with the Bureau of Prison's methodology: If the Bureau of Prisons is not mandated to apply previously earned (awarded) time credits until on or after January 20, 2022, why would it be mandated to apply time credits earned prior to January 22, 2022 at all? What about inmates discharged before application?

These complete failures of the system are described in Part IV. of this publication. Shockingly, there has been no press, public notice, or public outcry relative to this most recent Bureau of Prisons unofficial policy statement regarding untimely application of time credits. The policy is unofficial, because it is not contained on the Bureau of Prison's Website, but appears in multiple District Court cases nationally, beginning in the summer of 2020.

Matters Of First Impression-

All of the issues, disparities, and failures presented in this publication are being realized by inmates and other prison reform groups and scholars, monitoring these shortfalls. BOP issues generally result in split decisions in the District Courts nationally.

One thing seems clear, the majority of District Courts do not want to deal with a flood of time credit petitions, if they can avoid that predicament. Many liberal District Courts still do not want to deal with it.

The disparities and failures identified in this publication are over-ripe for *Mandamus* review, *Habeas Corpus* review, and Congressional review, now.

The Authors applaud the efforts of Senator Dick Durbin (D-IL), the primary author of the First Step Act, and Representative Jerry Nadler (D-NY) who have sponsored some very important continued First Step Act Legislation pending now in the 2021-2022 117th Congress. Look for something significant to pass with bipartisan support prior to the November, 2022 elections.

In that regard, Federal Sentencing Alliance has recommended changes be made to several substantive law provisions of the First Step Act, in order to close loopholes, such as those described in this publication.

The COVID-19 Pandemic-

The official launch date by the Bureau Of Prisons of Evidence-based Recidivism Reduction (EBRR) Programs and Productive Activities (PA) (on January 20, 2020) was only 52 days prior to the Declaration of National Emergency, COVID-19 Pandemic by President

Trump, on March 13, 2020. The Bureau of Prisons went immediately into medical lock down that remained for the rest of 2020 and into 2021, with no meaningful implementation of programs and activities occurring as a result, but time credit incentive programming did occur.

It is clear that the United States does not yet have the COVID-19 Pandemic under control yet, as evidenced by a resurgence of COVID-19 variant illnesses, hospitalizations and deaths, in the summer-fall of 2021. A large minority of the United States population still has not been vaccinated, or has refused to get vaccinated. There exists even civil unrest regarding one's right to refuse vaccination, while maintaining other perceived constitutional rights. COVID-19 is far from over, considering several virus mutations that have already occurred. It is axiomatic that COVID-19 spikes will impact pre- release time credit programming into 2022, especially those that require outside Vendor hosting at Bureau of Prisons facilities nationwide.

For the aforementioned reasons, calendar years 2019-2021 did not, and will not, result in the level, breadth, or depth of programming expected by inmates for any of those years. Inmates will undoubtedly fight to get 2019-2021 awarded time credits timely applied to their accounts, including 2019 time credits earned that the Bureau of Prisons refuses to recognize as valid.

Relay Race With A Rocky Start-

The First Step Act Of 2018 is akin to *a relay-race*, whereby various federal agencies must timely hand off a baton to the next runner in the race. Without the baton hand-off, the second runner cannot begin the race.

Such has been the case with Bureau Of Prisons utilization of *previously existing* recidivism reduction programs and production activities, during the preliminary phase in and expansion periods, and also in, "First Step Act Of 2018: Risk And Needs Assessment System" ("System") *actual* release and implementation.

There is simply no reason for 2019 time credit disparities, as Congress authorized immediate relief and immediate programs and activities incentives, as of December 21, 2018, and inmates earned credits in 2019.

The *ultra conservative* approach initially being planned for application of a fraction of time credits earned is both remarkable and skewed in the favor of the Department Of Justice. Quite frankly, the planned methodology is *ad hoc,* arbitrary and capricious, and only serves the Bureau of Prisons' interests.

It should be noted that thousands of recidivism reduction programs and productive activity Vendors rely upon incentive programming for livelihood. If inmates cannot earn meaningful pre-release time credits, incentive to engage in programming and activities could drop, and could wind up negatively effecting Vendors providing these services. That would be a tragedy.

Not A Neutral Playing Field-

Many were hopeful that the First Step Act Of 2018 would be implemented and applied with an even hand and on an equal playing field. Congress clearly intended for qualified inmates to immediately benefit from the Act, and to benefit to the maximum extent possible. The early warning signs presented in this publication cast doubt that certain aspects of the Act are being implemented or applied with an even hand or on an even playing field. If they were, they would not require litigation to compel a different result than the result that is happening now.

<u>Qualified inmates</u> means those inmates that are not unqualified, as described below.

An inmate serving a sentence for a conviction of one of the enumerated offense listed at 18 U.S.C. § 3632(d)(4)(D)(2019) is <u>not qualified</u> to engage First Step Act recidivism reduction programming or productive activities for time credits applied to reduce incarcerative sentence, pursuant to 18 U.S.C. § 3624(g)(2019).

PART II.

First Step Act of 2018: Risk and Needs Assessment System - Incentive Programming Implementation Delays, Disparities & Failures:

Introduction

The First Step Act Of 2018 ("Act") was signed into law by President Donald Trump on December 21, 2018, directing the Bureau Of Prisons to *immediately authorize* earned time credit incentives. 18 U.S.C. §§ 3621(h)(4)(6)(2019).

The Congressional intent of the Act was immediate time reduction credit relief for qualifying inmates. 18 U.S. C. § 3621(h)(4)(6)(2019) Pursuant to the Act, the Bureau Of Prisons ("BOP") was Congressionally mandated to utilize earned time credit incentive programs and activities, immediately on and after December 21, 2018, using previously existing recidivism reduction programs and productive activities already in use by individual BOP facilities, during the preliminary phase in, or expansion period. *Id.*

The BOP was then mandated to expand, vet and approved, evidence-based recidivism reduction programs and productive activities, within 210 days of December 21, 2018, during the initial phase in period, and release the complete "System" on or before January 19, 2019. 18 U.S.C. § 3632(a)(2019).

It is important to realize that prior to the First Step Act the Bureau of Prisons already had recidivism reduction programs and productive activities in use, and the Act merely authorized the Bureau of Prisons to use those previously existing programs and activities to award early release time credits to inmates during the initial phase in period; namely calendar year 2019.

The Attorney General's Office did not release a "First Step Act Of 2018: Risk And Needs Assessment System" [hereinafter "System"], or an "approved and vetted list" of "recidivism reduction programs" or "productive activities" [hereinafter "List"], on or before, July 19, 2019,[1] regardless of what Attorney General Barr

---

[1] On December 31, 2019, the Bureau Of Prisons published a document in the Federal Register titled "Good Conduct Time Credit Under The First Step Act". 82 FR 72274 (December 31, 2019) This document is a proposed BOP Rule change to 28 CFR 523 aka BOP-1032-P, that inter alia, recalculation of release date of inmates for good time credits, to mean 54 days of good time credits based upon the sentence imposed by the courts. *Id.* Noteworthy is this statement from the Summary Section thereof: "However, as provided in the FSA, this change will not be effective until the Attorney General completes and releases the risk and needs assessment system." *Id.* At 72274. This statement in sum and substance is an acknowledgment from the BOP that AG Barr had not released a risk and needs assessment system, as of December 31, 2019.

publicly announced. That statement was and remains false. Nobody seemed to notice, or ask where's the List.

Attorney General Barr did publish a document on July 20, 2019, titled "First Step Act Of 2018: Risk And Needs Assessment System" [hereinafter "RNA"] on the National Institute Of Justice[2] [hereinafter "NIJ"] Website.

This document was not a *risk and needs assessment system*, nor could it be, but rather, it is just a document titled "Risk And Needs Assessment System".

The First Step Act Of 2018 mandated that new evidence-based recidivism reduction programs be substantively *approved and vetted*, prior to release of

---

[2] The National Institute Of Justice or "NIJ" is an agency of the United States Department Of Justice, that is a department in the criminal division of the United States Attorney General's Office.

the "System"[3]. In other words, that the Attorney General's List of vetted and approved programs and activities had to exist prior to official release of the System. That did not occur. *See also n. 1, supra.*

Congress realized that the *system* could not be released without programs and activities being first

---

[3] Congress referred to the 'Risk And Needs Assessment System' simply as the "System", in 18 U.S.C. § 3632(a)(2019) and again in 18 U.S.C. § 3621(h)(1)(2019). As such, the term "System" means the new system developed, *vetted and approved* by the Attorney General, and not, previously existing programs and activities systems in place by the BOP prior to the First Step Act Of 2018. The distinction is that BOP had a system in place for recidivism reduction programming and productive activities programming prior to December 21, 2018, that is now being replaced by a newer vetted and approved "System" produced by the Attorney General's Office. Congress acknowledged the existence of previously existing evidence-based recidivism reduction programs and productive activities at any given BOP facility, as of December 21, 2018; and as such, acknowledged the previously existing systems in place by BOP, prior to enactment of the First Step Act Of 2018, as viable for incentive utilization during System phase in and System expansion periods. 18 U.S.C. §§ 3621(h)(1)(4)(6)(2019). As such, Congressional intent was immediate implementation of First Step Act time credit incentives during the preliminary phase in and expansion periods, and for all times on and after December 21, 2018.

approved and vetted within 210 days of December 21, 2018, and made that specific needs component a prerequisite to release of the system. *See* 18 U.S.C.§§ 3633(a)(3)(5) (2019)

> ("(a)...Prior to releasing the *System*...(3) identify the most effective evidence-based recidivism reduction programs;... (5) direct the Bureau of Prisons regarding-(A) evidence-based recidivism reduction programs;" *Id.*)

Attorney General Barr's July 19, 2019 document publicly released, a "Risk And Needs Assessment System", was in fact a prototype risk assessment tool called "PATTERN" (e.g. A prisoner assessment tool designed to assess risk of recidivism), subject to change, without ANY needs assessment system components listed, *per se*, as delineated in 18 U.S.C. § 3632(a)(b)(2019).

Initial PATTERN Tool (Prototype)-

It is not possible to re-compute how the numerous Ph.D.'s arrived at the actual cut points used in that schedule, because there is a disconnect between the logic and methodology flow cited and the final cut points derived. Nobody can recompute how those cut points were derived using the Attorney General's released System document; we tried.

Since the published evidence-based methodologies used to derive (e.g. recompute) initial cut points actually being utilized in the PATTERN prototype, cannot be independently verified from documents released to the public, there is no way for the public to verify whether those cut points utilized are based on evidence based methodologies or not.

Moreover, subsequent cut point changes cannot be checked either.

So, the complete System was not released until January 20, 2020, 6 months late. The entire System was then composed of the prototype PATTERN (risk) tool from July 19, 2019 coupled with the List (needs) component of the System released on January 20, 2020.

On January 20, 2020 a new PATTERN 1.2 tool was released making several substantive modifications to the original PATTERN tool, including cut points, but it was not immediately published by the BOP. Since there was no way to recompute how the original cut points were derived, there is no way to recompute how the PATTERN 1.2 tool cut points are derived either.

Then on January 20, 2021 the National Institute

of Justice published a further document online titled *2020 Review and Revalidation of the First Step Act Risk Assessment Tool.* That is an annual public acknowledgment that NIJ believes that the existing risk assessment tool is still valid, as required by the First Step Act. *See* 18 U.S.C. § 3631(b)(4)(2019).

PATTERN version 1.2 remains the most current version of the PATTERN risk assessment tool at this time, as found here online: https://www.bop.gov/inmates/fsa/docs/the-first-step-act-of-2018-risk-and-needs-assessment-system-updated.pdf

Generally speaking, a qualified inmate is entitled to earn early release earned time credits during the entire period of his or her incarcerative sentence, on and after December 21, 2018. 18 U.S.C. § 3621(h)(6)(2019).

The problem with entitlement is that it is benign

when the same person does not have the right to meaningfully complain to a sympathetic ear when their entitlement expectations falls short.

Mandatory Authority Granted To The Bureau Of Prisons To Use Then Existing Incentive Programming-

In calendar year 2019, the BOP did not use its (mandated) authority to utilize earned time credit incentives for successful completion of previously existing recidivism reduction programs and productive activities, as directed by Congress under the First Step Act Of 2018[4]. 18 U.S.C. §§ 3621(h)(1)(4)(6)(2019)

There are two distinct BOP (mandatory)

---

[4] Moreover, in 2019, the Attorney General did not release to the public an approved and vetted list of recidivism reduction programs or productive activities, that was due as part of the publicly announced Risk And Needs Assessment System proffered on July 19, 2019, but only contained a prototype risk assessment tool.

authority provisions enumerated in the First Step Act Of 2018, relative to BOP's duty to utilize and/or implement early release earned time credit programs and activities.

The disconnect was and is in use of the word "may" by Congress in various First Step Act Provisions, interpreted by the Bureau of Prisons really to mean "you can't force me".

The first (mandatory) authority is found at 18 U.S.C. §§ 3621(h)(1)(4)(6)(2019) (hereinafter "immediate relief provisions" or "previously existing programs and activities"), and the second mandatory authority is found at 18 U.S.C. § 3621(h)(1)(hereinafter "system implementation provisions" or "RNA" or "system").

Both of those enumerated duties are *cumulative*.

These duties are cumulative because, BOP had a duty to immediately utilize, for inmate earned early release time credits, previously existing recidivism reduction programs and productive activities, as of December 21, 2018; and that BOP had a separate duty to implement the Attorney General's *new System,* at least by January 20, 2020, the same cutoff date for initial PATTERN assessments to have been completed for all inmates.

With those dates in mind, the BOP breached two separate Congressionally mandated duties under the First Step Act Of 2018, the first one on and after December 21, 2018 and the second one on and after January 20, 2020.

From December 21, 2018 to January 20, 2020, the Bureau Of Prisons opted to *just wait* to receive an *approved and vetted* list of programs and activities *released to the public* from the Attorney General's Office, instead of utilizing its (mandated) authority to utilize already existing incentive programming for time credits during the preliminary phase in period.[5] The Attorney General's "List" was finally released on

---

[5] In 2019 several inmates filed Petitions For Writs Of Mandamus and/or Petitions For Writs Of Habeas Corpus- sounding in Mandamus, in the District Of South Carolina, against the Bureau Of Prisons relating to First Step Act Of 2018 immediate application of *good conduct* time credits. The D.S.C. Judges in Denying these Petitions, either on *ripeness* issues or *technical deficiencies* relating to failure to exhaust administrative remedies, recognized that BOP's *duty apply good conduct time credits* was connected to AG Barr's *duty to release a risk and needs assessment system by July 19, 2019*, and that until AG Barr releases a risk and needs assessment system, that the BOP's duty to apply good conduct time credits does not arise. *See Blake v. Bureau Of Prisons*, 2:19-cv-0818-RMG (D.S.C. May 13, 2019); *Brown v. Warden Of FCI Williamsburg*, 8:19-cv-00546-HMH-JDA (D.S.C. March 25, 2019); *Dailey v. Bureau Of Prisons,*1:19-cv—662-RMG-SVH (D.S.C. April 24, 2019); *Griffin v. Bureau Of Prisons,*0:19-cv-00642-CMC-PJG (D.S.C. May 10, 2019); *Ransom v. Bureau Of Prisons,* 1:19-cv-00703-HMH-SVH (D.S.C. April 24, 2019); and *Robinson v. Bureau Of Prisons,* 1:19-cv-00648-HMH-SVH (D.S.C. April 24, 2019). As previously noted, AG Barr has stated publicly that the Risk And Needs Assessment System was released on July 19, 2019.

January 20, 2020. See RNA, p. 71 ("When that review[6] is complete, no later than January, 2020, *a full list of the approved programs will be posted* on the BOP's website." *Id.*) Folks, that *List* was the needs component of the System that was Congressionally mandated to be released within 210 days of December 21, 2018! 18 U.S.C. § 3633(a) (2019) The general public did not notice or complain about this release shortfall at all.

The enumerated duties of the Attorney General and Bureau Of Prisons under the First Step Act Of 2018 are both *circular* and *cumulative*. The First Step Act itself mandates that the Attorney General and the Director of the Bureau Of Prisons, *inter alia*, coordinate

---

[6] As previously stated, that Attorney General "review" was Congressionally mandated to have been completed before release of the system on or before July 19, 2019, not arbitrarily completed by sometime in "January 2020".

their activities, presumably so these unexplained (latent) time delays won't happen. 18 U.S.C. § 3631(a)(2019)

The duties are *circular*, because *some of* BOP's duties arise 180 days after the release of the Risk And Needs Assessment System - "System", but the BOP denied that a Risk And Needs Assessment System was released by the Attorney General, as of December 31, 2019, *supra,* n. 1. Why didn't anybody complain about that BOP Federal Register notice disparity either?

It is uncertain at this point what impact the 6 month time lag had on the Bureau of Prisons internal policies regarding these issues, that are largely a secret endeavor, invisible to the public view. On occasion there is a window to some of those secrets by examining arguments made in the District Court, representing stated policies of the Bureau of Prisons, regardless of whether those policies stated in court are official, unofficial, publicly noticed, or otherwise confidential.

The District Court For The District Of South Carolina, *supra, n. 5*, acknowledged the connectivity of those two separately stated duties, as *circular*. If there is no hand off, the second runner is stymied.

For instance, the 6 month List delay could have been used as justification for WHY the Bureau of Prisons now does not want to award any incentive programming time credits for ANY time periods through January 20, 2020.

It seems clear that the BOP on December 31, 2019 postured itself in the Federal Register in order to later deny that it's duties for implementation of early release earned time credit programs and activities, were delayed, because the Attorney General did not release a Risk And Needs Assessment System on July 19, 2019, *supra, n. 1*.

But, Attorney General Barr stated publicly that the RNA was released on July 20, 2019, by virtue of the published document titled the same, *supra*.

The duties are *cumulative*, because both the Attorney General's Office and the Director of the Bureau Of Prisons were Congressionally mandated to be in "consultation" relative to due dates and mandatory duties of agency members. 18 U.S.C. § 3631 (a)(2019)

It is remarkable that as of December 31, 2019, the BOP publicly claimed that the system was not yet released, which can only be viewed as an attempt to push back it's own mandatory implementation, award, and application dates, pursuant to 18 U.S.C. § 3621(h)(1) (2019). That is exactly what the Bureau of Prisons has already done, that is "pushed back" it's perceived (mandatory) credit award and credit application dates. Those timing push backs are discussed in greater detail later on in this publication. The old adage "timing is everything" could not be truer for inmates hoping to benefit from early release time credits before they are naturally time served.

Moreover, aside from the BOP's statement made in the Federal Register at 82 FR 72274 (December 31, 2019), *supra, n. 1*, the BOP has not otherwise publicly stated that the Attorney General's Office didn't release a complete Risk And Needs Assessment System, on July

19, 2019. So it was just a whisper in order to make an official record and a muffled whisper at that.

BOP Ignored the Act's Mandate For Immediate Utilization of Earned Time Credit Incentives, Pursuant To 18 U.S.C.§§ 3621(h)(4)(6)(2019)-

The Bureau Of Prisons *should have* utilized First Step Act Of 2018 earned time credit incentives *immediately on and after December 21, 2018,* by permitting inmates to earn First Step Act early release time credit incentives, through successful completion of *previously existing programs and activities*, but did not.

These matters are cited in Section 102 of the Act, in subsection (4), thereof, and codified in 18 U.S.C. § 3621(h)(4)(2019).

In Section 102, Subsection (4), First Step Act "May" Means "Must"
Welcome to Congressional Semantics-

What is semantics anyway?

"se·man·tics
/s 'man(t)iks/
noun

   the branch of linguistics and logic concerned with meaning. There are a number of branches and subbranches of semantics, including formal semantics, which studies the logical aspects of meaning, such as sense, reference, implication, and logical form, lexical semantics, which studies word meanings and word relations, and conceptual semantics, which studies the cognitive structure of meaning.

   the meaning of a word, phrase, sentence, or text."

- courtesy of Oxford Languages .

Hypothetical Use Of Semantics-

For instance, if someone said "You *must* cut the lawn in the next half hour, and you *may* use the lawn mower", logically "you may use the lawn mower" is a grant of authority. It is not logical or feasible to cut the lawn in the next half hour without use of the lawn mower, so it is disingenuous to pretend that your use of the lawn mower to cut the lawn in a half hour is discretionary on your part. Moreover, even it you did not use the lawn mower, deciding that you had discretion not to use the lawn mower offered, the lawn would still need to be cut in half an hour. So, even if you hired a third party lawn service to cut the lawn, exercising your discretion not to use the lawn mower available, the lawn would still need to be cut in the time period stated.

Such was the case with the Bureau of Prisons. They were mandated to provide immediate and full incentive programming as of December 21, 2018 forward, and they were granted authority to utilized pre existing risk tools, and preexisting programs and activities for incentive programming during the initial phase in period.

It is disingenuous for the Bureau of Prisons to argue that they were given discretion to deny all early release time credit incentive programming for calendar year 2019, vis a vis Congressional authority to use preexisting tools and programs to make it happen.

In Section 102 Subsection (4) of the Act, the operative word "may" does not mean "may", but rather means "shall" and "must", relative to the Act's Grant of authority to the Bureau Of Prisons, to utilize earned time credit incentives during the preliminary phase in, or preliminary expansion period, commencing on and after December 21, 2018.

Congressional intent for the First Step Act was to provide immediate relief to qualifying inmates. 18 U.S.C. §§ 3621(h)(1)(4)(6)(2019) Indeed, many other provisions of the Act had immediate effect.

The word "may" used in the Act's Section 102: "(4) Preliminary expansion of evidence based recidivism reduction programs and authority to use incentives..", codified at 18 U.S.C. § 3621(h)(4)(2019), did not create a precatory, optional, elective, or avoidable duty for the Bureau Of Prisons. The word "may" in this provision, using standard rules of judicial interpretation, and federal caselaw, including the reading of this subsection *in pari materia* with the Act *in toto*, and also considering Congressional intent for the Act, means "shall" and "must", but not "may".

The Bureau of Prisons, conversely interprets the word "may" as though it has authority under the First Step Act to squash all early release time credits earned prior to the date the List was release by Attorney General Barr on January 20, 2020. That is an aberration and a falsehood.

To date, few have complained about that notion, which makes no logical sense from a plain reading of the First Step Act time credit provisions *in toto*.

Congress would not mandate something in the

first part, only to give the Bureau of Prisons authority to un-mandate itself in the second part. Congress wanted the lawn cut, and got no lawn cut in 2019.

Section 102(4) of the First Step Act Of 2018, and 18 U.S.C. § 3621(h)(4), Word "May" Really Means "Must", as "May" Merely Grants Authority To BOP To Utilize Previously Existing Programs And Activities

The Word "May"-

"While the word "may" in a statute creates a presumption of some degree of discretion, this presumption can be *defeated by indications of legislative intent to the contrary or by obvious inferences from the structure and purposes of the statute. Cortez Byrd Chips, Inc. v. Bill Harbert Constr. Co.*, 529 U.S. 193, 198-199 (2000) (The word "may" in a statute "usually implies some degree of discretion, *but this common-sense principle of statutory construction . . . can be defeated by indications of legislative intent to the contrary or by obvious inferences from the structure and purpose* *of the statute"); Usmani v. U.S. Attorney Gen.,* 483 F.3d 1147, 1150-1151 (11th Cir. 2007) (The word "may" in a statute creates a presumption of some degree of discretion, but "this presumption *can be defeated by indications of legislative intent to the contrary or obvious inferences from the structure and purpose of the statute*") (*quoting DirectTV, Inc. v. Brown,* 371. F.3d 814, 817 (11th Cir. 2004)); *see also Myles v. State, 602 So. 2d 1278,* 1281 (Fla.1992) ("We realize, as the court below noted, that the statute in question uses the word `may' in talking about electronic communications. However, it is settled that the word `may' is not always permissive, but may be a word of mandate in an appropriate context."); *Comcoa, Inc. v. Coe,* 587 So.2d 474, 477 (Fla. 3d DCA 1991)("Specifically, an imperative obligation is sometimes regarded as imposed by a statutory provision notwithstanding that it is couched *57 in permissive, directory, or enabling language.") Such is the case here." *Miccosukee Tribe of Indians of Florida v. United States*, 04-cv-21448-GOLD/ McALILEY (U.S.D.C. S.D. Fla. July 29, 2008)(Order Granting Summary

Judgment, pps. 29-31)[Italics added].

The above cited cases speak of factors to be considered for interpreting "may" to really mean "must". Those factors are: 1.) Legislative intent to the contrary; 2.) Obvious inferences; and 3.) The structure and purpose of the statute. These factors are also designed to be a "common sense principle of statutory construction". *See generally Miccosukee Tribe of Indians of Florida, supra*. Moreover, all statutory changes must be considered *in pari materia* with one another, in order to determine overall Congressional intent. *Id.*

The word "may" in Section 102(4) of the Act, and 18 U.S.C. § 3621(h)(4)(2019) means that the Bureau Of Prisons was given Congressional authority, or permission, to utilize previously existing programs and activities during the preliminary expansion period for purposes of immediate earned time credit incentives; not that the Bureau Of Prisons was given *permissive authority to defeat the tenets of the First Step Act,* by denying earned time credit incentives in 2019, through complete failure to offer or utilize previously existing earned time credit incentive programs and activities during the entirety of 2019; simply through inaction.

The Word "System"-

In *Shapiro v. Valmont Industries, Inc.,* 982 F.2d 237, 242 (7th Cir. 1992), a case involving interpretation of a commercial lease, the Court interpreted the meaning of "sprinkler system". The Court first noted that the word was used in the singular "system" as opposed to "systems", meaning one system as opposed to multiple systems. *Id.* Next the Court stated: "Viewed in isolation, the word "system" is just as easily construed to mean the entire sprinkler system or one of its three sections." *Shapiro v. Valmont Industries, Inc.*, 982 F.2d 237, 242 (7th Cir. 1992)

Relative to Patent terms interpretation "[a]bsent an express intent to impart a novel meaning, claim *terms* take on their ordinary meaning. *See Renishaw PLC v. Marposs Societa' Per Azioni,* 158 F.3d 1243, 1249, 48 USPQ2d 1117, 1121 (Fed. Cir. 1998). " *Elekta Instrument v. O.U.R. Scientific,* 214 F.3d 1302, 1307 (Fed. Cir. 2000)(Italics added)

"The word "system" itself imports a unity of purpose as well as an entirety of operation" *Board of*

Education of City of Ardmore et al. v. State, 26 Okla. 366, 371 (Okla. 1910).

The word "system," as employed in the [State Of California] constitution, means an organized plan or scheme in keeping with which the constituent parts thereof are rendered similar and are connected and combined into one complete, harmonious whole, and it necessarily imports both a unity of purpose and entirety of operation. (Welsh v. Bramlet, 98 Cal. 219, [33 P. 66]; Board v. State,26 Okla. 366, [109 P. 563]; State v. Riordan, 24 Wis. 484.) *Coulter v. Pool*, 187 Cal. 181, 192 (Cal. 1921) "As previously indicated, uniformity means consistency, resemblance, sameness, a conformity to one pattern. In this resemblance, in this sameness, in this conformity of a class to one pattern, consists the uniformity of system which is essential to the creation and continuity of a uniform system." *Id.*

Regarding incentive time credits for qualified inmates, Congress mandated a singular System both Risk and Needs components, with early release programming incentives, intended to be both enticements and entitlements. These statutory entitlements created substantive rights for qualified inmates.

The components of the Risk And Needs Assessment System, Congressionally mandated to have been released on or before July 19, 2019, are delineated with specificity in 18 U.S.C. § 3632(a), and contain Inmate's Needs Assessment and Programming components and inmate entitlements thereto, in Subsections (1)(3)(5)(6)(7) and (8).

The Word "Implementation" Or "Implement" And Its Usage In The Act-

Merriam-Webster defines the word "implementation" as "..an act or instance of implementing something : the process of making something active or effective".

As part of First Step Act Of 2018 mandates, and within 180 days after release of the Attorney General's Risk And Needs Assessment System, the Bureau Of Prisons was Ordered to "implement", "complete the initial intake risk and needs assessment for each prisoner", and "begin to assign prisoners to appropriate evidence-based recidivism reduction programs based on that determination" [of the newly released *System*], simultaneously "..while prisoners are participating in and completing the effective evidence-based recidivism reduction programs and productive activities." [of previously existing BOP programs and activities, required for immediate implementation on and after December 21, 2018] 18 U.S.C. § 3621(h)(1)(A)(C) (2019); *See also* 18 U.S.C. §§ 3621(h)(4)(6)(2019).

"When determining the legislature's intended meaning of a statutory word, it also is appropriate to consider the surrounding words pursuant to the canon of construction *noscitur a sociis*[7]. McCoy v. Commissioner of Public Safety, 300 Conn. 144, 159, 12 A.3d 948 (2011). By using this interpretive aid, the meaning of a statutory word may be indicated, controlled or made

---

[7] Merriam-Webster definition– *noscitur a sociis*. : a doctrine or rule of construction: the meaning of an unclear or ambiguous word (as in a statute or contract) should be determined by considering the words with which it is associated in the context. *Id.*

clear by the words with which it is associated in the statute. *State v. Roque,* 190 Conn. 143, 152, 460 A.2d 26 (1983)." *State v. Lafleur,* SC 18757, at *11 (Conn. Sep. 28, 2012)

In the First Step Act Of 2018, Congress used the terms "implementation" and "implement" associated with *expansion* of programs and activities released under the System released by the Attorney General, due on July 19, 2019, and not associated with the Bureau Of Prisons mandatory authority to engage inmates with previously existing- ongoing recidivism reduction programs and productive activities already in use at BOP facilities nationwide, as of December 21, 2018, during the phase in, or preliminary expansion periods.

It is clear that the Bureau Of Prisons did not

implement the Attorney General's Risk And Needs Assessment System released on July 20, 2019, because the BOP stated (as embedded) in the Federal Register that there was no System released as of December 31, 2019, *supra, n. 1.*

It is also clear that the Bureau Of Prisons did not utilize previously existing recidivism reduction programs and productive activities already in place at various BOP facilities nationwide, to engage inmates in early release earned time credit incentives in 2019, during the preliminary phase in period, that continues to this day due to the failure of the Attorney General Barr to release a timely usable System. The release of half of a prototype system on July 19, 2019 did not constitute release of a full usable System.

The First Step Act Of 2018, Sec. 102 (4) states:

"(4) PRELIMINARY EXPANSION OF EVIDENCE-BASED RECIDIVISM REDUCTION PROGRAMS AND AUTHORITY TO USE INCENTIVES. - Beginning on the date of enactment of this subsection, the Bureau of Prisons *may begin to expand any evidence-based recidivism reduction programs and productive activities that exist* at a prison as of such date, *and may offer* to *prisoners who successfully participate in such programs and activities the incentives and rewards described in subchapter D." Id.; See also 18* U.S.C. § 3621(h)(4)(2019).

Why did it take an extra 6 months for Attorney General Barr to release a 6 page List? Nobody knows and nobody complained about it, it just was.

The First Step Act Of 2018, Sec. 102 (6) states:

"(6) REQUIREMENT TO PROVIDE PROGRAMS TO ALL PRISONERS; PRIORITY.-The Director of the Bureau of Prisons *shall provide all prisoners with the opportunity to actively participate in evidence-based recidivism reduction programs or productive activities, according to their specific criminogenic needs, throughout their entire term of incarceration. Priority for participation in recidivism reduction programs shall be given to medium-risk and high-risk prisoners, with access to productive activities given to minimum-risk and low-risk prisoners."* Id.; See also 18 U.S.C. § 3621(h)(6) (2019)

Senator Richard Durbin and Senator Chuck Grassley, Letter to Attorney General Merrick Garland, May 5, 2021 Regarding First Step Act Earned Time Credits Disparities and Failures-

The text of Durbin-Grassley Letter to new Attorney General Merrick Garland, dated May 5, 2021, is cited as supporting many of the studied conclusions drawn in this publication. The letter is especially noteworthy, considering the lack of federal caselaw on these issues presented, together with new unofficial Bureau of Prison policies, and Rule changes, that keep cropping up as time progresses.

"May 5, 2021

The Honorable Merrick Garland
Attorney General
U.S. Department of Justice
950 Pennsylvania Avenue, NW
Washington, DC 20530

Dear Attorney General Garland:

We respectfully request that you direct the Bureau of Prisons (BOP) to expeditiously revise the proposed rule published on November 25, 2020, regarding earned time credits authorized by the First Step Act of 2018 (FSA).

As proposed, the rule severely limits the incentive structure designed to increase program participation and would undercut the effectiveness of the FSA. We ask that you reevaluate and amend the rule consistent with the statute's goals of incentivizing and increasing program participation to reduce recidivism. The proposed rule undermines the FSA's incentive structure in several respects. First, by defining a day as eight hours of programming the rule greatly restricts the ability to earn credits. Under the FSA, eligible inmates "shall earn 10 days of time credits for every 30 days of successful participation in evidence-based recidivism reduction programming [EBRR] or productive activities [PAs]." While not statutorily defined, the plain meaning of a day of participation is every calendar day during which a person successfully participates in an EBRR or PA, with the length of participation determined by the program. Instead, the proposed rule defines a day as "one eight-hour period" of a completed EBRR or PA. Using this definition, an inmate who participates in a program one hour a day for eight days would earn just one "day" of participation under the FSA. Given the limited programs offered and the duration and frequency of programs, earning enough time credits to meaningfully reduce prison time would be nearly impossible under this definition.

Second, the proposed rule allows credits to be earned only for programs that were assigned and completed after January 15, 2020, more than two years after the FSA's date of enactment. The FSA does not require BOP to limit earned time credits to completion of assigned programming. BOP's inclusion of this limitation in the proposed rule is particularly troublesome because BOP has not developed an effective needs assessment, as required by the FSA. Under the proposed rule, inmates would not be rewarded for self-identifying needs and voluntarily participating in programming. The proposed rule also, without authority or explanation, prohibits credits for programs completed before January 15, 2020, when the FSA allows for credits based on all programming completed after the statute's enactment on December 21, 2018.

Third, the FSA directs that all eligible federal prisoners in BOP custody shall earn credits for program participation, but the proposed rule would exclude prisoners in residential reentry centers (RRCs) or home detention. Because prisoners in RRCs and home detention are in BOP custody, the rule is contrary to the FSA. In fact, the FSA specifically anticipated that prisoners on home detention would continue to participate in programming by listing program participation as one of a few authorized reasons prisoners may leave home while on detention.

Finally, we are concerned that the proposed rule's penalties are unduly harsh. The rule proposes that inmates may lose earned time credits "for violations of prison rules, or requirements and/or rules of an [EBRR or PA]," applying the same procedures used for loss of good time credits. Especially when combined with the time required to earn credits under the proposed rule, the penalty for violations would be too severe. For example, one unexcused absence from a work assignment could result in the loss of 30 days of earned credits, although earning those credits would require completing 720 hours of programming. The rule also imposes penalties for violations of program requirements, rather than just violations of "prison rules or [EBRR or PA] rules," as the FSA requires, suggesting that failure to fulfill the requirements of a program not only could result not only in a failure to earn time credits for participation, but also the loss of credits previously earned.

While losing hard-earned credits would be easy, the rule makes restoring credits too difficult. The FSA simply requires "a procedure to restore time credits that a prisoner lost as a result of a rule violation, based on the prisoner's individual progress." However, the proposed rule would only allow for restoration after "clear conduct for at least four consecutive risk and needs assessments." These assessments may only be completed annually, so it could take a prisoner at least four years to restore lost credits, longer than the average sentence.

For these reasons, we ask that you direct BOP to expeditiously revise the proposed rule consistent with the comments above. Establishing robust programming and a fair system to earn time credits is critical to meeting the FSA's goal of reducing recidivism.

Thank you for your time and consideration. We look forward to your prompt response.

Sincerely,

Richard J. Durbin
Chair
U.S. Senate Committee on the Judiciary

Charles E. Grassley
Ranking Member

U.S. Senate Committed on the Judiciary"

See Press Release May 5, 2021 and Durbin-Grassley Letter Linked to that press release found here:

https://www.grassley.senate.gov/news/news-releases/durbin-grassley-press-doj-to-strengthen-first-step-act-rule-on-earned-time-credits-to-incentivize-rehabilitation

Many of the identical substantive disparities listed in the Durbin-Grassley Letter of May 25, 2021 to Attorney General Merrick Garland, *supra,* were brought to the attention of the Congress by Federal Sentencing Alliance on January 31, 2020, by written letter with publication appendices.

On July 28, 2021 Federal Sentencing Alliance wrote Senator Durbin a letter, suggesting for consideration, that one critical substantive amendment be made to the First Step Act earned time credit provisions, 18 U.S.C. § 3632(d)(4)(A) (i)(ii), for inclusion into S. 1014, The First Step Implementation Act of 2021. The suggested amendment, four simple words and two commas: ", or any part thereof," added to subsections (i) and (ii) would ensure that inmates got credit for 1 day of program or activity participation for every 1 day participating in a program or activity (not just hours spent in the classroom). If embraced by Congress, that single amendment would solidify the original intent of Congress enacting time credit incentives under the First Step Act, for the Bureau of Prisons to award time credits based on days of program participation. *See also* Durbin-Grassley Letter, *supra,* regarding this same issue.

      In 2019 Senator Dick Durbin (D-IL) accused the

Bureau of Prisons of intentionally undermining the First Step Act in other matters, as found here:

https://www.durbin.senate.gov/newsroom/press-releases/durbin-to-bop-director-why-is-doj-undermining-the-first-step-act

While Durbin's Press Release is unrelated to time credits per se, it goes further by publicly stating that the Bureau of Prisons is undermining the First Step Act in general, as of the date of the Press Release. *Id.*

> **November 25, 2020 Bureau of Prisons published Earned Time Credit (Proposed Rules) in the Federal Register, Pushing Back Intended Credit Applied Dates, while simultaneously Moving Forward Intended Qualifying Credit Award Dates, Contrary to the First Step Act, and Congressional Intent-**

The Bureau of Prisons has official stated that it will not award time credits for programs and activities completed prior to January 15, 2020, contrary to the express provisions of the First Step Act itself. [See Federal Register/Vol. 85, No. 228/Wednesday, November 25, 2020, pps. 75268-75271]["FSA Time Credits may only be earned for successful completion of an Evidence-Based Recidivism Reduction program and Productive Activity assigned to the inmate based on the inmate's risk and needs assessment, and only for those successfully completed on or after January 15, 2020." *Id.* At p. 75269]

The Bureau of Prisons has also now officially stated that it defines "a day" of earned time credit programming to mean "8 hours" of in class programming, as opposed to the number of "days" enrolled in any program or activity to successful completion:

"A "day" is a unit defined as one eight hour-period of a successfully completed Evidence-Based Recidivism Reduction program or Productive Activity. The Bureau derives its proposal for earning FSA Time Credits from 18 U.S.C. 3632(d)(4)(A)(i), which indicates that inmates"shall earn 10 days of Time Credits for every 30 days of successful participation in evidence-based recidivism reduction programming or productive activities."

As authorized by the FSA in 18 U.S.C. 3632(d)(4)(A)(ii), inmates may earn an additional five days of FSA Time Credits for every thirty "days" (with a "day" defined as one eight-hour-period) of participation in a successfully completed Evidence-Based Recidivism Reduction program or Productive Activity that is assigned to the inmate based on the inmate's risk and needs assessment if the inmate is at a minimum or low risk for recidivating and has had no increased risk of recidivism over the most recent two consecutive assessments conducted by the Bureau of Prisons.

FSA Time Credits may only be earned for successful completion of an Evidence-Based Recidivism Reduction program and Productive Activity assigned to the inmate based on the inmate's risk and needs assessment, and only for those successfully completed on or after January 15, 2020.

Additionally, an inmate may only earn FSA Time Credits after the date that inmate's term of imprisonment commences, which is defined as when the inmate arrives or voluntarily surrenders at the facility where the sentence will be served. Further, FSA Time Credits can only be earned while an inmate is in a Bureau facility, and will not be earned if an inmate is in a Residential Reentry Center or on home confinement." *Id.* At 75269; *See also* Durbin-Grassley Letter, *supra.*

It appears that the Bureau Of Prisons has thus far, also successfully manipulated the timing of when it is mandated to apply time credits awarded to an inmate's time credit account, arbitrarily fixing that date to be January 20, 2022, See *infra,* Part IV; contrary to First Step Act provisions requiring immediate benefits realized to foster overall incentive programming goals.

Although the Bureau of Prisons has no official stated policy published on this issue, that arbitrary January 20, 2022 date has been successfully argued in

U.S. District Courts as a drop dead, mandated date, for applying time credits previously awarded, but not applied to an inmate's time credit account, in a multitude of federal court cases nationally.

In other words, inmate time credit applied petitions are being denied by District Courts based on *ripeness grounds*, in addition to other stated reasons. *See infra, U.S. v. Martinez* line of cases.

This arbitrary to be "applied date" proffered by the Bureau of Prisons, and accepted by the majority of U.S. District Courts to date, means that thousands of inmates nationally will successfully complete recidivism reduction and productive activities programming, post January 20, 2020, only to be released from the Bureau of Prisons as time served, prior to January 20, 2022.

PART III.

DOJ /BOP EARLY RELEASE TIME CREDIT INCENTIVES PROGRAMMING IMPLEMENTATION AND PLANNED TIME CREDIT AWARDS PLANNED FOR PRE-RELEASE CUSTODY DETERMINATION *IN PARA FLAGRANTE DELICTO*, VIOLATES THE FIRST STEP ACT AND EFFECTIVELY RENDERS 18 U.S.C. § 3632(d)(4)(2020) *ULTRA VIRES*

Introduction

There is a *gaping hole* between the actual earned time credit incentives that inmates believe they will earn to be applied toward pre-release custody, pursuant to 18 U.S.C. § 3632(d)(4)(2020), verses what the Bureau Of Prisons has set into motion that they will earn. It is clear that the BOP's intent is to eviscerate application of earned early release time credit *benefits* to inmates, essentially rendering the lion's share of time credits that

Congress intended inapplicable to reduce any inmates incarcerative sentence meaningfully. Time credits are used to reward inmates with pre-release, when the balance of their incarcerative sentence is equal to time credits earned. Time credits do not reduce an imposed sentence, *per se*, but rather reduce the incarcerative portion of the sentence only.

The BOP released the *approved and vetted* listing of evidence based recidivism reduction programs and productive activities on January 20, 2020, six months late, *supra*. It is this List itself that revealed Attorney General Barr's intentions relative to setting a *tiny number of hours (not days)* to be awarded for successful completion of programs and activities, but then, not making these widely available anyway. Under

AG Barr's planned implementation system, inmates won't be able to collect more than a few months of time credits, if that, over an elongated time period. These anomalies are not caused from the law, *per se,* but are solely based upon AG Barr's restrictive interpretation of Congressional intent, and Attorney General Barr's creative use of this common sense equation: One "day" = "24 hours", prior to November 25, 2020 (just from looking at the four corners of the vetted and approved List of recidivism reduction programs and productive activities approved on January 20, 2020, *supra*), and One "day" = "8 hours" on and after November 25, 2020 (official policy from looking at the Federal Register/Vol. 85, No. 228/Wednesday, November 25, 2020, pps. 75268-75271).

This one example is indicative of overall time credit disparities and failures that keep cropping up presenting the crux of this legal anomaly; being the goal post keeps moving after the ball is kicked.

As previously stated, see Senator Richard Durbin published a Press Release titled *Durbin To BOP Director: Why Is DOJ Undermining The First Step Act?* found here:

https://www.durbin.senate.gov/newsroom/press-releases/durbin-to-bop-director-why-is-doj-undermining-the-first-step-act

The Operative Statute- 18 U.S.C. § 3632(d)(4) (2019):

"(4) Time credits.

(A) In general. A prisoner, except for an ineligible prisoner under subparagraph (D), who successfully completes evidence based recidivism reduction programming or productive activities, shall earn time credits as follows:

(i) *A prisoner shall earn 10 days of time credits for every 30 days of successful participation in evidence based recidivism reduction programming[8] or productive activities[9].*

(ii) A prisoner determined by the Bureau of Prisons to be at a minimum or low risk for recidivating, who, over 2 consecutive assessments, has not increased their risk of recidivism, shall earn an additional 5 days of time credits for every 30 days of

---

[8] It is axiomatic that one is involved in "programming" by signing up and completing work assigned. An inmate is successfully involved in "programming" from day to day throughout the program, not hour by hour, in class only. AG Barr's use of semantics violates the spirit of the Act, because Barr's interpretation renders earned time credit benefits mostly ineffective as a means to gain meaningful pre trial release credits. Moreover this is hardly an incentive under the AG Barr schematic. Congress does not use the term "hours" in the Act relative to earning time credits applied to pre-release custody. That is AG Barr's creation.

[9] The word 'programming" is not defined in Federal caselaw relating to recidivism reduction programs or productive activities. Congress did not define the term "programming" either in this context. The common meaning of "programming" in this context is: 'the action or process of scheduling something'. *See Oxford Dictionary*

successful participation in evidence based recidivism reduction programming or productive activities." *Id.*

What the Bureau Of Prisons has in mind for implementation and application of earned early release time credit incentives can be best explained by using the following analogy.

Assume that someone earns a four year college degree and is asked how many years they attended college, to which they would respond four years. AG Barr would say that is not true, because the college student was only *in college* a few hours per day.

Four Year College Degree Hypothetical-
A Literal Reading Of 18 U.S.C. § 3632(d)(4)
(2020) Would Lead to this Result-

If full time college (e.g. 5 courses per semester, or 10 courses per year, for each of four years) were considered productive activities, and one earned a four year college degree while incarcerated, one would expect these time credit incentives applied toward early release:

> 48 months (e.g. four year college degree earned)
>
> x 1/3 (10 days per month applied to early release time credits)
>
> = 16 months earned early release time credits (=480 days @ average of 30 days/month)
>
> =4 months per year earned time credits (=120 days per year time credits)

That is how Congress intended for early release time credit incentives to work, e.g. if an inmate was engaged in full time productive activities[10] that they

---

[10] Congress did not define what "programming" means, or what basis or extent of participation in "programming" entitled an inmate to an early release time credit of 10 days per month. The Act is vague in that regard, however, it cannot be the intent of Congress to pass an Act that is *benign* in effect.

could earn 10 days per month while engaged in, and successfully completing productive activities. That is the *literal reading* of 18 U.S.C. § 3632(d)(4)(2020).

DOJ/BOP Reading Of 18 U.S.C. § 3632(d)(4)(2019)-

Same hypothetical using BOP's methodology-

Assuming the same facts relating to the above lucky inmate who earns a four year college degree in 48 months, and believes that he or she is enrolled in full time productive activities. The DOJ/BOP, having a *conservative interpretation* of 18 U.S.C. § 3632(d)(4)(2020), would apply earned time credits:

40 courses (= a four year college degree)

x 3 hours per week class time (for 3 credit courses each)
<u>x 16 weeks</u> (course term 4 months)

= <u>1920 hours</u> (in class)

<u>x 1/3</u> (based on the fraction 10 days for every 30)

640 potential hours to be awarded (at 1/3)

<u>/8 hours</u> = one day, *per* Federal Register/Vol. 85, No. 228/Wednesday, November 25, 2020, pps. 75268-75271, "Rule" announced by the Bureau of Prisons. *Id.* ["/8" means divided by the number 8]

= <u>80 days</u> earned time credits awarded total

Not the 16 months contemplated by the First Step Act, as used in this hypothetical example.

/4 years = 20 days per year of incarceration.

According to the logic of and Rules implemented by the Bureau of Prisons, assuming that an inmate with a minimal risk of recidivism PATTERN 1.2 assessment were able to engage in and complete a full 4 year college degree in custody, that inmate would only be awarded 2

2/3 months of pre release time credits, using the methodology and logic presently in place by the Bureau of Prisons in 2021. This logic represents a deliberate obstructive interpretation, or bastardization, of the intent of Congress related to these issues. *See* Durbin-Grassley Letter in Opposition, *supra*.

The Bureau of Prison methodology does not incorporate any time credits given for inmate program and activity preparation outside the classroom preparation, which is a material aspect of any meaningful program or activity, and without which, successful completion of that program or activity would not be possible. A normal college setting requires 3 hours of outside the classroom preparation for every hour of class time. If that were not the case, few would graduate from college.

The AG Barr Fallacy *Sounding In Semantics*: This was the AG Barr Reading of the Law using Semantics-

Since AG Barr released the *approved and vetted listing*[11] of evidence based recidivism reduction programs and productive activities, these things have become apparent from a cursory study of the listing itself:

1.) AG Barr only intends to award earned time credits for *actual class time only*. Most of the classes and activities offered are a couple hours or less, and for a

---

[11] Prong #1 of this Fugazi was to release the List six months late, further crippling inmates to figure Prong #2 out. Prong #2 here will be figured out by inmates shortly when they meet with their Counselors feeling great about participating in programming for 3 weeks having earned 1 week of early release time credits, only to be told that they really earned 4.5 hours, and will eventually get 1.5 hours applied, one day.

limited time period.

2.) There is no way to engage programs and activities full time; and even if there were a means to do so full time, that would only be 8 hours per day, and not 24 hours per day of time, and still not equal to 1 day of programming participation.

3.) No time credits are planned to be awarded for time enrolled into programs and activities, or for self study or class preparation time, but only for actual time that the programs and activities are in session, and computed as "hours" and not "days".

4.) No time credits are planned to be awarded for any programs or activities completed prior to January 20, 2020.

5.) Time credits awarded based on 8 hours in

class = one day of award, further subjected to the 1/3 Rule, are not planned to be applied to an inmate's time credit account, until on or after January 20, 2022.

6.) Another specific example below, using a program vetted and approved from the List, regarding an inmate "English Student" highlights Attorney General Barr's interpretation of earned time credits to be awarded, being "hours" not "days".

The Approved And Vetted List Of Programs And Planned Application Of Credits

Interestingly, aside from the Durbin-Grassley Letter, *supra,* and Federal Sentencing Alliance as first published in January, 2020 in a prior related Edition of this publication, no other organizations have negatively reported on these issues to date; no prison reform organizations and no activists; no watchdog groups and no news organizations.

The Inmate English Student Productive Activity Example Cited From "The List"

Here is one example of earned time credits that *would be applied* for recidivism reduction programs and productive activities, once they become available for engagement[12]:

    PA Name: English-as-a-Second Language

    Duration: Depends on inmate progress

    Frequency: Minimum of 1.5 hours/day

---

[12] See January 20 2020 BOP Release titled: "Evidence-based Recidivism Reduction (EBRR) Programs and Productive Activities (PA)" [hereinafter "the List"], released by publication on the Bureau Of Prisons Website, as found here: https://www.bop.gov/inmates/fsa/docs/evidence_based_recidivism_reduction_programs.pdf

On January 15, 2020, AG William Barr publicly stated that the Bureau Of Prisons would be releasing the programs and activities list on the BOP Website. The list released is the list that AG Barr was supposed to release by July 19, 2019, but did not.

Hours: 500

Availability: All BOP institutions

Purpose: Education, Work

Analysis: At 1.5 hours per day this inmate would spend 333.33 days to learn English and be awarded 20.8 days of early release time credits to be applied to pretrial release, but only on and after January 20, 2022. (500 hours /8 hours per day /3 (award fraction based on 10 days for every 30 days of participation) = 20.8 days); not the 111.11 days of earned time credits that the inmate is expecting to earn from a literal reading of 18 U.S.C. § 3632(d)(4)(2020), (e.g. 333.33 days x 1/3 = 111.11 days).

It is helpful to restate the operative provision which states: "(i) A prisoner shall earn 10 days of time credits for every 30 days of <u>successful participation in evidence based recidivism reduction programming or productive activities</u>." *Id.*

According to AG Barr's logic, the English student is "in and out" of "programming" daily; "in" while in class, and "out" when out of class. The only way for AG Barr not to award time credits is to *deem* that the inmate is not engaged in programming unless the inmate is sitting in class. That is an uncommon view of how program participants engaged in any program are viewed in general. Normal use of the term "programming" in this context, connotes a course of conduct with requirements, that is a 24/7 engagement endeavor, not just hourly while *in class.*

AG Barr gives this inmate no credit for all the

studying that will be involved outside of the classroom, which is preposterous. It is common knowledge that out of class time studying comprises 3x the amount of time spent in class, otherwise one will fail the class.

What AG Barr has *subtly done* here is the following-

- The Congress directed 10 days per 30 days involved in successful completion of "programming", pursuant to 18 U.S.C. § 3632(d)(4)(2020). The English Student Inmate is engaged in "programming", which for him or her is a full time endeavor.

- The English Student Inmates only gets rewarded 10.5 hours per week (1.5 hours per day x 7 days) time credits, when there are 168 hours in a week.

- The Congress directed "days" of time credits, but somehow AG Barr has turned programming "days" into programming "hours", via the use of *semantics*.

- Notwithstanding that the Congress directed credit for "days" of programming, AG Barr has *assigned an arbitrary number of hours*[13] per day, and then used that arbitrary number of hours per day to derive a total number of possible hours that can be earned, per program or activity. The total hours awarded per program or activity are set in stone, for the most part, in the List.

- The English Student Inmate *only benefits from a tiny fraction of the number of days he or she was actively engaged in programming.*

---

[13] None of these things are mentioned in any released Needs And Assessment System as mandated by the Congress. Assigning an arbitrary number of earned hours without any empirical authority or basis, is the same practice that AG Barr employed in creating the PATTERN assessment tool.

- Moreover, BOP programs and activities are not widely available, and where they are available, it is only for a portion of the day or week; literally a few hours here and there.
- AG Barr has *ipso facto* made it impossible for a single inmate to earn meaningful early release time credits, through these *ultra conservative* implementation and application tactics.
- Earned time credits under BOP's current (hourly) credit plan for any inmate nationally would only constitute a *minutia* of actual days that an inmate spent incarcerated, which is surely not the intent of Congress, *via* enactment of the First Step Act Of 2018. Bear in mind that an inmate is sentenced to a number of months and days, not sentenced to a number of hours.

18 U.S.C. § 3621(h)(6)(2020), Section 102 First Step Act Of 2018, states:

"(6) REQUIREMENT TO PROVIDE PROGRAMS TO ALL PRISONERS; PRIORITY.-The Director of the Bureau of Prisons shall provide all prisoners with the opportunity to actively participate in evidence-based recidivism reduction programs or productive activities, according to their specific criminogenic needs, *throughout their entire term of incarceration*. Priority for participation in recidivism reduction programs shall be given to medium-risk and high-risk prisoners, with access to productive activities given to minimum-risk and low-risk prisoners." *Id.*(Italics added)

First Step Act SEC. 602. Home confinement for low-risk prisoners, states:

"Section 3624(c)(2) of title 18, United States Code, is amended by adding at the end the following: The Bureau of Prisons shall, to the extent practicable, *place prisoners with lower risk levels and lower needs on home confinement for the maximum amount of time permitted under this paragraph[14]." Id.*

Remedies/BOP Time Credit Anomaly Issues-

These anomalies represent separate BOP Request Issues, because they relate to how much time will be awarded, and then, when those time credits will actually be applied. So these issues are substantively different from the first BOP Request.

This *earned time credit implementation and application issue* could be a *Mandamus issue*, an *ultra vires law issue,* a waiver issue, a petition for *writ of habeas corpus* issue, and an *18 U.S.C. § 3582(c)(1)(A)*

---

[14] In order to benefit from this provision, one needs to have earned time credits in the bank. This provision is benign to the extent there are no time credits, or minimal time credits, in the earned time credits bank. By stifling an inmate's ability to earn time credits, and then further stifling an inmate's ability to earn meaningful full time credits, AG Barr has effectively dissected all of the beneficial provisions of First Step Act time credit incentives programming, morphing them into something never intended by Congress.

(2020) application of time credits issue in the months and years to come, because it appears that the BOP is not going to award or apply earned time credits for early release meaningfully, or timely, to actually benefit any inmate released prior to January 20, 2022.

Attorney General Barr set the stage for that "hours awarded for completion" battle that is apparent from a cursory review of the four corners of the *approved and vetted list* of evidence based recidivism reduction programs and productive activities released by the BOP on January 20, 2020; the List.

No BOP Rule Federal Register Press-

Normally when the Bureau Of Prisons is planning on making a rule", here implementation and application of program and activity credits to an inmate's pre-release custody consideration under the First Step Act Of 2018, the BOP would create a planned "rule" and publish that planned "rule" in the Federal Register, inviting comments from legal pundits that can examine the planned "rule" under a microscope, and comment. That procedure is not only peer review procedure, but gives people effected a chance to intelligently object to the planned rule. That procedure did not happen here, until November 25, 2020, 23 months after the First Step Act was enacted. What happened in those first 23 months?

As such, the writing was always on the wall that implementation delays, reduced time credits awards, and untimely time credits applied issues, were all being *silently set into motion*, while also being skewed in favor of the Bureau of Prisons.

Having said that, the Authors recognize that the BOP is in a difficult position with these issues, as they were initially directed by Attorney General Barr on all of these underlying core issues that still remain in place.

Federal Sentencing Alliance is calling on Attorney General Merrick B. Garland to fix these cancerous tumors embedded into Bureau of Prisons official and unofficial policies related to earned time credits awarded and applied by predecessor Attorney General William Barr.

The BOP is a federal agency within the Department Of Justice umbrella, that the Attorney General heads. These disparities and failures can be corrected now by Attorney General Garland, as evidenced by a cursory reading of the Durbin-Grassley Letter cited, *supra.*

The BOP may have started out in 2019-2020, between a rock and a hard place with some of these issues, to the extent it was controlled by Attorney General Barr (e.g. the Attorney General's Office making official and unofficial Policy for the Bureau Of Prisons, as opposed to the Bureau Of Prisons making implementation and application "Rules" for itself).

Additionally, the failure to publish intended Rules in the Federal Register truly flies in the face of *transparency*, which is a major goal of the First Step Act Of 2018. *See infra,* Part IV,, relative to the arbitrary time credit application date of January 20, 2022, representing the unofficial policy of the Bureau of

Prisons on that issue.

Lastly, it does not appear that there is any *empirical data or behavioral basis*, supporting the arbitrary assignment of a very small number of hours per day or week, and then computing the total number of hours to be awarded for completion of a program or activity considering only classroom hours.

In sum, the Bureau of Prisons earned time credit incentive programming implementation, the List details of time credits planned to be awarded, and the arbitrary January 20, 2022 time credit to be "applied date", *infra,* Part IV,, all look arbitrary and capricious. First Step Act programs and activities are supposed to act as incentives, but the incentives portrayed will never be realized under current methodology in place.

Where time credit incentives are reduced *arbitrarily*, the First Step Act Of 2018 fails. Where inmates successfully complete programs and activities with time credits arbitrarily withheld, the First Step Act fails. Where the Bureau of Prisons makes Rules that fly in the face of Congressional intent, that should have been interpreted from a literal reading of the four corners of the First Step Act itself, the Act fails. In so many words, the Bureau of Prisons has constructively amended substantive provisions of the First Step Act, by promulgating Rules to the contrary, without authority.

There is no doubt that these issues will create an onslaught of Inmate Requests and District Court Petitions in the months and years to come.

PART IV.

FIRST STEP ACT EARLY RELEASE TIME CREDITS EARNED IN 2020-2021 MAY NOT BE TIMELY APPLIED TO AN INMATE'S TIME CREDIT ACCOUNT UNTIL ON OR AFTER JANUARY 22, 2022:

More Semantics: Permissive Authority verses Mandatory Authority Arguments Made

This Section is extremely troubling to the Authors, as it should be to the readers of this publication and the public at large.

The premise stated below is that, just because an inmate earns pre-release time credits under the First Step Act, it is not mandatory that the same inmate benefit from those time credits earned (from 2019-2021) through timely application of those time credits by the Bureau of Prisons to reduce an inmate's incarcerative sentence.

The Bureau of Prisons has convinced the majority of United States District Courts reviewing this particular issue, that the Bureau of Prisons is not mandated under the First Step Act to apply earned time credits, to actually reduce an inmate's incarcerative sentence, until on or afer January 20, 2022.

Thousands, if not tens of thousands of inmates completing First Step Act incentive programming and activities during the period 2019 through 2021, will inevitably be released from the Bureau of Prisons without receiving any time credit awards. If you think that proposition is preposterous, it is not, as delineated below. This is the wrong result at the wrong time for the wrong stated reasons by the majority.

A Word About Bureau of Prison Policy-

During the early stages of the First Step Act, the official Bureau of Prisons policy was made or approved by Attorney General William P. Barr, as the Attorney General's Office was responsible for releasing several core milestone documents under the First Step Act, representing major changes on a multitude of fronts.

Then, there are the official BOP policies that were and are published on the Internet, and/or included as Proposed Rules in the Federal Register, that are conveniently incomplete much of the time.

Then, there are the unofficial policies of the Bureau of Prisons that act as accepted Rules that are neither contained in a milestone document released by the Attorney General's Office, contained on the Bureau of Prisons Website, or noted in the Federal Register whatsoever.

At times, unofficial Rules of the Bureau of Prisons are meted out from District Court caselaw, examining any specific issue, and founded upon an argument made by an Assistant United States Attorney zealously representing his or her Client, the United States.

Such was the case with the Bureau of Prisons accepted unofficial policy statement that it is not mandated, pursuant to the First Step Act to actually apply time credits awarded until on or after January 20, 2022, *infra*.

This unofficial policy is not only atrocious, but flies in the face of fundamental fairness for inmates that earnestly embraced incentive programming to reduce their own recidivism propensities, or just to improve themselves while incarcerated.

The Authors believe that inmates should be deemed to have a constitutional right to timely application of earned time credits, similar to rights already possessed by inmates to timely application of "good time" credits, pursuant to federal law.

What Is The Genus Of The Bureau Of Prisons Argument For The January 20, 2022 To Be "Applied" Drop Dead Date?-

18 U.S.C. § 3621(h)(2021) reads:

"(h) IMPLEMENTATION OF RISK AND NEEDS ASSESSMENT SYSTEM.-

(1) IN GENERAL.-*Not later than 180 days after the Attorney General completes and releases the risk and needs assessment system (referred to in this subsection as the "System")* developed under subchapter D, the Director of the Bureau of Prisons shall, in accordance

with that subchapter-

(A) *implement and complete the initial intake risk and needs assessment for each prisoner* (including for each prisoner who was a prisoner prior to the effective date of this subsection), regardless of the prisoner's length of imposed term of imprisonment, and begin to assign prisoners to appropriate evidence-based recidivism reduction programs based on that determination;

(B) *begin to expand the effective evidence-based recidivism reduction programs and productive activities it offers and add any new evidence-based recidivism reduction programs and productive activities necessary to effectively implement the System*; and

(C) *begin to implement the other risk and needs assessment tools* necessary to effectively implement the System over time, *while prisoners are participating in and completing the effective evidence-based recidivism reduction programs and productive activities.*

(2) PHASE-IN.-*In order to carry out paragraph (1), so that every prisoner has the opportunity to participate* in and complete the type and amount of evidence-based recidivism reduction programs or productive activities they need, and be reassessed for recidivism risk as necessary to effectively implement the System, *the Bureau of Prisons shall-*

(A) provide such evidence-based recidivism reduction programs and productive activities for all prisoners before the date that is 2 years after the date on which the Bureau of Prisons completes a risk and needs assessment for each prisoner under paragraph (1)(A); and

(B) develop and validate the risk and needs assessment tool to be used in the reassessments of risk of recidivism, while prisoners are participating in and completing evidence-based recidivism reduction programs and productive activities." Id. [Italics added]

To summarize, the Bureau of Prisons interprets these provisions as follows, based upon arguments made in District Courts related thereto, *infra*:

1.) The Risk and Needs Assessment System was released on July 19, 2019.

2.) Initial Risk and Needs Assessments were completed for all Bureau of Prisons Inmates on or before January 15, 2020.

3.) The Bureau of Prisons is not mandated to provided any First Step Act incentive programs or productive activities to any particular inmates, until it is mandated to ensure programs and activities available to all inmates; on or before, January 15, 2022.

4.) The fact that some inmates may have earned early release time credits prior to January 15, 2022, but not yet awarded or applied to their time credit accounts, still does not mandate the Bureau of Prisons to award time credits earned until on or after January 15, 2022.

The Authors specially note that the *January 20, 2022* date being *bantered around* and cited in multiple U.S. District Court cases below, is an error standing alone, because the proper date that should have been used for the Department of Justice arguments should have been January 15, 2022, e.g. two years following the date all federal inmates received their first PATTERN risk assessment, *supra*. The operative calculation date, the on or before date that all inmates had already received their first PATTERN assessment was January 15, 2020, as published on the Bureau of Prisons Website, not January 20, 2020, the date that the vetted and approved List of programs and activities was released by Attorney General William P. Barr, *supra*.]

The Minority U.S. District Court Opinion-

The minority United States District Court view is painstakingly set forth by the Honorable Renée Marie Bumb, United States District Judge for the District of New Jersey, in the case of *Goodman v. Ortiz*, Case No.: 1:20-cv-07582-RMB (Aug. 25, 2020).

District Court Judge Renée Marie Bumb should get an award for not being afraid to do the right thing, notwithstanding that the majority of other District Court Judges rejected this precedent in their jurisdictions, *infra*.

"Petitioner [Rabbi Aryeh Goodman], a federal inmate at FCI Fort Dix, alleges that the Federal Bureau of Prisons

("BOP") has failed to apply his "Earned Time" credits for "Evidence-Based Recidivism Reduction Training" under the First Step Act, 18 U.S.C. § 3632(d)(4) (A), a recently enacted statute aimed at assisting prisoners' reintegration into society. Petitioner contends that the BOP should have given him credit for his participation in the training program and he should have therefore been released on July 5, 2020. (Pet., Dkt. No. 1, Petr's Aff., Dkt. No. 1-2.) *The BOP disagrees, arguing that its obligationto apply Earned Time credits does not take effect until the end of the phase-in period, which is January 15, 2022." Goodman v. Ortiz*, Case No.: 1:20-cv-07582-RMB (Aug. 25, 2020) [Italics added][Later changed to January 20, 2022 in the majority opinions, *infra.*]

"On August 28, 2019, Chief Judge Wolfson sentenced Petitioner to an eighteen month term of imprisonment. (Declaration of Christina Clark ("Clark Decl."), Ex. A, Dkt. No. 4- 3.) Assuming Petitioner receives all good time credits available to him, but none of the Earned Time credits awarded under the First Step Act, which are at issue here, his projected release date is January 20, 2021." *Id.*

Aryeh Goodman's alleged earned time credits included certain time credits allegedly earned from 2019 programs. [*See Habeas Corpus Petition*, 1:20-cv-07582-

RMB [DE 1, p. 14]

Goodman also alleged he was entitled to 50% of earned time credits applied, based upon receipt of a second subsequent "low" recidivism risk assessment received from his Case Manager. *See* 18 U.S.C. § 3632(d)(4)(2019).

The *Goodman* Court went through a few milestone events in the case-

"• A Case Manager "determined and [Programming] Activities" for Petitioner at meetings held on November 26, 2019 and January 20, 2020. (Pet. Aff. ¶¶ 2.2, Dkt. No. 1-2; Ex. 1, Dkt. No. 1-1 at 1-2);

• These assignments met the requirements of the Act, and the Case Manager explicitly confirmed to Petitioner that they qualified under the Act. (Pet. Aff. ¶¶ 3-3.2, Dkt. No. 1-2; Ex. 2, Dkt. No. 1-1 at 3-9);

• Petitioner successfully participated (and continues to participate) in this programming. (Id.)

• Petitioner has accumulated 240 days of credit, which

under 18 U.S.C. §§ 3632(d) (4), 3635 serves to reduce his sentence by 120 days. (Pet. Aff. ¶¶ 4.4; 5.1-5.3, Dkt. No. 1-2.)

• If Petitioner's days of credit are applied upon program completion, under 18 U.S.C. §§ 3632(d)(4), 3635, he should have been released on July 5, 2020. (Pet. Aff. ¶ 4.4, Dkt. No. 1-2.)

Thus, because the BOP does not dispute that Petitioner earned the time credits, Petitioner seeks immediate application of those credits under the First Step Act.

The BOP makes two arguments in opposition to Petitioner's request for habeas relief. First, it contends that Petitioner failed to exhaust his administrative remedies. Second, it argues []that the BOP is not required to award any PATTERN earned credit until the two-year phase-in period under the statute has expired, to wit, January 15, 2022." *Id.*

The *Goodman* Court's Conclusion-

"The BOP's position that a prisoner can complete the PATTERN program before January 15, 2022 with no benefit to the prisoner is contrary to the statutory language, not to mention the unfairness of such a result.

Therefore, *the Court concludes that Petitioner is entitled to habeas relief. The Court will direct the BOP to immediately apply Petitioner's Earned Time credit of 120 days in an accompanying Order.* [] Date: 16 August 25, 2020 s/ Renée Marie Bumb" *Id.*

The Authors specifically note that the Bureau of Prisons *Rule change* of November 25, 2020 was promulgated after the *Goodman* case was lost. Additionally Goodman was awarded days, not hours, for program participation. Lastly, Goodman also received some 2019 incentive programming time credits, applied by the District Court.

Here is a summation of the reasons why Petitioner Rabbi Aryeh Goodman was a Rock Star related to his filed earned, but not timely applied, time credits habeas corpus petition:

1.) The United States did not argue, *per se*, that Petitioner lacked standing to file the petition, pursuant to the time credits provisions of the First Step Act, but merely that administrative appeals processes were not exhausted. That was a good thing.

2.) The United States took the position that the Bureau of Prisons could withhold applying time credits earned arbitrarily, just because it can, which looked inherently unfair on its face. There is really no way around that proposition: it looks unfair, because it is unfair.

3.) The United States arguments regarding January 15, 2022 truly look reaching, because the fact that the Bureau of Prisons actually places an inmate into incentive programming successfully completed, has no bearing on other inmates not placed into programming, because they did not qualify for one reason of another.

Any argument that could be made that it is not fair to apply credits earned by some, because other inmates did not earn credits or qualify for credits would appear ludicrous.

4.) Rabbi Goodman got 2019 time credits into the mix, where the Bureau of Prisons is now specifically denying any time credits will be awarded or applied for any 2019 programs or activities.

5.) Rabbi Goodman got full days of program participation awarded and applied by the District Court, as opposed to a *minutia of hours* that would have been ultimately awarded by the Bureau of Prisons, based on its obscure and arbitrary application standards.

6.) The application of earned time credits to the Rabbi Goodman's time credit account was actually meaningful in his case. It was meaningful because the District Court made it meaningful, under First Step Act authorities. Out of an 18 month sentence, the Rabbi was awarded half of his program participation days by the District Court, and he effectively shortened his incarcerative sentence by 4 months = 120 days overall.

7.) Rabbi Goodman's case shows the proper way that First Step Act incentive programming time credits are supposed to be timely applied, to do any good for an inmate, under the First Step Act.

The *Goodman* Case Initial Rollout-

As would be expected, other federal inmates nationally filed similar petitions for writ of habeas corpus with their individual District Courts, only to be denied by the majority of District Court Judges ruling on substantially similar petitions, as the one filed by Rabbi Aryeh Goodman.

The Authors believe that the District Courts' denials could be based upon other reasoning that has nothing to do with the four corners of the petitions presented to them, *infra.* Many liberal Districts also.

The Majority View, Stated in *U.S. v. Martinez*-

There is a certain truth to the fact that a District Court Judge can always write an opinion to support the position it wants to take regarding any issue presented, within the doctrine of stare decisis. This one is no different.

Forgetting the obvious for a moment, the majority opinions are written in such a way to stymie, block, humble and prevent, an onslaught of similar time credit petitions for writ of habeas corpus from being filed by federal inmates nationally. Onslaught = tens of thousands, if not more.

Interestingly, many of the same Circuits that found an *emergency jurisdiction* of sorts to grant petitions for compassionate release, based upon extraordinary and compelling reason stated as "COVID-19" during calendar year 2020, denied petitions for awarded, but not applied, early release time credits for a multitude of reasons that look wholly one sided.

Didn't the Bureau of Prison waive any claimed right it had not to timely apply earned time credits until after January 20, 2020, by actually placing an inmate into approved incentive programming and productive activities that were successfully completed by an inmate in 2019-2021? The award promise was made before time credits were earned. What good are time credits to be applied after an inmate has already been released?

In other words, when the United States argues that the Bureau of Prisons is not mandated to place inmates into incentive programming and activities until on or after January 20, 2022, the reply to that should be "but, the Bureau of Prisons did". There is no justiciable reason to withhold application of time credits earned, except because the District Courts apparently gave the Bureau of Prisons license to do just that, in the majority opinions stated below.

The Authors specially note that some of these opinions state January 20, 2022 as the "applied" mandate date, while others state January 22, 2022; but none state

January 15, 2022, two years following completion of all first PATTERN risk assessments, completed January 15, 2020. For that reason it appears that the Bureau of Prisons cannot even correctly compute the correct "applied" mandate date supporting its arguments made in various District Courts.

The majority of United States District Courts have ruled that it is not mandatory for the Bureau Of Prisons to apply early release time credits awarded for successful completion of Department of Justice approved recidivism reduction programs and/or productive activities, pursuant to 18 U.S.C. § 3632(4), at any time prior to January 22, 2022; the last day of the "phase in period" requiring full implementation of early release programming, pursuant to the First Step Act.

The majority interpretation makes First Step Act 18 U.S.C. § 3632(4) *ultra vires* for thousands of inmates that have been, and will be, released prior to January 22, 2022, without having any early release earned time credits applied to reduce their incarcerative sentences under the First Step Act for 2019-2021 programs and activities earnestly completed in good faith.

The majority interpretation can also mean, *ipso facto,* that the Bureau of Prisons may never be mandated to award early release earned time credits under the First Step Act, earned by inmates prior to January 22, 2022, because the majority interprets that inmates have no standing to complain about time credits at all to the District Courts directly.

The open question remains: What happens to

time credits earned, but not applied during the period January, 2019 through January, 2022?

Here is a rundown of some United States District Court cases that specifically considered and analyzed the minority opinion very eloquently stated by the Honorable Renée Marie Bumb, United States District Judge for the District of New Jersey, in the case of *Goodman v. Ortiz*, Case No.: 1:20-cv-07582-RMB (Aug. 25, 2020), and trounced that case as valid precedent.

At the time of this publication these cases represent the majority view on this issue nationally, and specifically rejecting the minority view of *Goodman v. Ortiz, supra*:

United States v. Martinez, No. 5:12-cr-00769-EJD-1 (N.D. Cal. June 14, 2021);

Depoister v. Birkholz, Civ. 21-684 (ECT/BRT) (D. Minn. July 8, 2021);

Cornell v. Bennett, 4:21-CV-04056-RAL (D.S.D. July 21, 2021);

Kennedy-Robey v. Warden, FCI Pekin, No. 20-cv-1371 (C.D. Ill. Mar. 2, 2021); and

Novotny v. Yankton FPC, 4:21-CV-04074-RAL (D.S.D. July 21, 2021).

Here is a snippet from the *United States v. Martinez* opinion that sets the tone for the majority rulings cited above:

"D. Ripeness

Petitioner contends that he is entitled to 360 days of credits he has earned under the First Step Act, and therefore he should be released immediately. The Government counters that the Bureau of Prisons has until January 22, 2022 to fully phase in the First Step Act time credits.

The Court agrees with the Government. The First Step Act is intended to be phased in. The Bureau of Prisons has until July 19, 2019 to develop a risk and

needs assessment system; until January 15, 2020, to initially assess each inmate's risk and needs; and until January 15, 2022 to complete a full assessment of each inmate, phase in programming, and provide recidivism reduction programs and productive activities for all inmates. See 18 U.S.C. § 3632(a), 3621(h)(2)(A), (B). But the statute does not expressly require the Bureau of Prisons to begin awarding earned time credits during the phase-in period. Cohen v. United States, No. 20-CV-10833 (JGK), 2021 WL 1549917, at *2-3 (S.D.N.Y. Apr. 20, 2021) (finding that claim is not ripe because BOP is not required to award earned time credits during the phase-in period). Other courts across the nation have considered the issue and agree with the Government as well. See, e.g., Kennedy-Robey v. FCI Pekin, 2021 WL 797516, at *4 (C.D. Ill. Mar. 2, 2021); Hand v. Barr, 2021 WL 392445, at *5 (E.D. Cal. Feb. 4, 2021) (report and recommendation); Llewlyn v. Johns, 2021 WL 307289 (S.D. Ga. Jan. 29, 2021); Herring v. Joseph, 2020 WL 3642706, at *1 (N.D. Fla. July 6, 2020).

Petitioner relies exclusively on Goodman v. Ortiz, 2020 WL 5015613 (D. N.J. Aug. 25, 2020). In Goodman, the court acknowledged that the First Step Act does not explicitly provide a date by which the Bureau of Prisons must apply earned time credits, but concluded that Goodman was entitled to immediate application of earned time credits because the statute "does require a 2-year phase-in, not only of participation in the programs, but of incentives for participation in the programs." *Id.* Although there is some logic to phasing in programs and earned time credits concurrently, that is not what the statute provides. The First Step Act sets intermediate deadlines for achieving certain tasks during the phase-in period, but is conspicuously silent regarding *5 applying earned time credits during that period.

III. CONCLUSION Accordingly, the petition for a writ of habeas corpus is DENIED. IT IS SO ORDERED.

Dated: June 14, 2021

/s/_____

EDWARD J. DAVILA
United States District Judge"

United States v. Martinez, Case No. 5:12-cr-00769-EJD-1 (N.D. Calif. June 14, 2021).

The *Martinez* majority opinion synopsis ignores all First Step Act provisions to the contrary, as well as the sound logic, fundamental fairness, and lawful authorities cited in *Goodman v. Ortiz, supra*.

Sadly, the *Martinez* Court should have just stated the real underlying reasons for the Court's denial of Martinez's petition, that could have looked something like this [hypothetical start]: "We cannot grant the instant petition, because if we do, tens of thousands of similar petitions may be filed by inmates nationally flooding the District Courts with time credit applied habeas corpus petitions. At the present moment in time, the Court will deny the petition based on a ripeness issue, but on and after January 22, 2022, the Court may reexamine the First Step Act provisions closer, and thereafter deny any future petitions made, based upon lack of standing, not specifically provided by the First Step Act." [hypothetical end]

Specially note that the *Martinez* Court cited February 22, 2022, not even February 20, 2022 like some of the other Districts; much less the real operative date of January 15, 2022 [e.g. the full implementation drop dead date], as argued by the Bureau of Prisons in the *Goodman v. Ortiz case, supra.*

As previously stated, this is not an even playing field and the goal post keeps moving after the football is kicked.

In the Authors opinion, the *Martinez* line of cases ignores all contrary provisions of First Step Act authorities and mandates, Congressional intent, and the spirit of the Act *in toto*, as though those things do not exist. Those decisions do not reflect a thorough examination of both sides of the law on these matters of first impression.

Had the Bureau of Prisons argued that inmates lacked standing under the First Step Act to bring time credit disparities to the District Court, *per se*, and argued that issue thoroughly and completely, perhaps that might have passed the sniff test. The *Martinez* line of cases just represent a *dump button* without sound legal basis.

The majority opinions give license to the Bureau of Prisons not to apply any First Step Act pre-release time credits to any inmate's time account, at the sole discretion of the Bureau of Prisons, until on or after January 20-22, 2022.

The majority opinions ignore violations of fundamental fairness, good faith and fair dealing, other basic human rights, and substantive rights conferred by the First Step Act. The Bureau of Prisons promised inmates (hourly) time credit awards for successful completion of approved programming and productive activities, as delineated on the face of the 6 page List, *supra,* with the captions "hours awarded for completion". The programs and activities were earnestly embraced and successfully completed by qualified inmates. Inmates completed their part of the bargain. Hours were awarded. But, now the *Martinez* majority opinion line of cases states that its okay for the Bureau of Prisons to withhold application of time credits rightfully earned under the First Step Act, rendering earned time credits for many-valueless.

If that does not look like [fill in the blank] in the inducement related to First Step Act time credit incentive programming by the Bureau of Prisons, the Authors would be loathe to opine what does.

These decisions will negatively effect thousands of inmates that earnestly embraced incentive time credit programming under the First Step Act, that will now be denied application of pre-release time credits by the Bureau of Prisons, before they are time served discharged in the normal course.

One has to wonder if the *Martinez* majority opinion line of cases are merely trying to forestall tens of thousands of pro se habeas corpus petitions from flooding federal District Courts, based on the failure of the Bureau of Prisons to timely apply prison time credits earned during the extended period January, 2019 through January, 2022.

Cumulative Effect of Implementation Disparities, Time Credit Award Disparities, and Time Credit Application Failures, and Current Efforts To Fix The Broken System-

Early release time credit programming under the First Step Act has been bastardized by the Bureau of Prisons to such an extent that it now resembles a *Trojan horse*; that is, it has morphed into something different than what it publicly appears to be.

Senator Dick Durbin (D-IL) and Representative Jerry Nadler (D-NY) are trying to fix some of the problems identified in this publication related to time credit incentive programming. They are also eager to supplement and amend related U.S. Code provisions to foster First Step Act and prison reform in a variety of substantive and meaningful ways.

The 2021 Legislation proposed, to date, does not

fix inequalities present with either (the amount of) earned early release time credits or the timely application of those credits. On the other hand, Attorney General Merrick Garland can fix the Bureau of Prisons inequitable time credit award and application Rules simply by Ordering the Bureau of Prisons to do so; hence, the Durbin-Grassley Letter to Attorney General Merrick Garland dated May 25, 2021 requesting those and other things. Whether or not Attorney General Merrick Garland embraces those requests or not remains to be seen.

Certain of the prior time credit disparities originally identified by Federal Sentencing Alliance in January, 2020, were repeated in the Durbin-Grassley Letter to Attorney General Merrick Garland, dated May

25, 2021, *supra*.

The Authors believe that program participation should be awarded based upon days of program and activity participation, not just hours, as delineated in the minority opinion, *Goodman v. Ortiz, supra*. Should that not be the case, there will never be any meaningful application of earned time credits under the First Step Act going forward. *See also* the May 25, 2021 Durbin-Grassley Letter, *supra,* supporting that same proposition.

The Term *Trojan Horse-*

Tro·jan Horse
/ˈtrōjən hôrs/
noun
noun: Trojan Horse; plural noun: Trojan Horses

   a hollow wooden statue of a horse in which the Greeks concealed themselves in order to enter Troy.

   a person or thing intended secretly to undermine or bring about the downfall of an enemy or opponent.

"the rebels may use this peace accord as a Trojan horse to try and take over"

Computing

a program designed to breach the security of a computer system while ostensibly performing some innocuous function.

- definitions courtesy of Oxford languages.

Getting back to Senator Richard Durbin's Press Release accusing the Bureau of Prisons of undermining the First Step Act, if true, why do you suppose that happened under the direction of Attorney General Barr?

The 2021-2022 117th Congressional Session-

Senator Richard Durbin (D-IL) and Representative Jerry Nadler (D-NY) are fully aware of Bureau of Prisons' shenanigans and will be trying to straighten them out in the 2021-2022 117th Congressional Session.

Here is a short list of current First Step Act of 2018 related Congressional legislation that has been introduced and is pending at the time of this publication:

S. 312 COVID–19 Safer Detention Act of 2021, sponsored by Senator Dick Durbin (D-IL).

H.R. 3669 COVID–19 Safer Detention Act of 2021, sponsored by Representative Jerry Nadler (D-NY).

S. 1014 First Step Implementation Act of 2021, sponsored by Senator Dick Durbin (D-IL).

Here is a short synopsis of some of the major provisions in the above cited Bills pending:

S. 312 COVID–19 Safer Detention Act 2021-

S. 312 and H.R. 3669 are the identical Bills in the U. S. Senate and U.S. House pending at this time:

Major Changes To the Second Chance Act of 2018 (Pilot Program) and compassionate release re: COVID-19 would become an automatic extraordinary and compelling reason for compassionate release, for CDC high risk qualified inmates.

1. Modification to the Second Chance Act 34 U.S.C. § 60541 (Pilot Program) for elderly or terminally ill offenders seeking immediate transfer to home detention once incarcerated. Provides authority for eligible elderly or terminally ill inmates to immediately request transfer to home detention with the Bureau Of Prisons ("BOP"). Provides standing to inmates to request

court review after, the earlier of, exhausting the BOP administrative review processes (that can take up to a year), or the passage of 30 days with no BOP Warden Response to the inmate's initial request. Provides District Court jurisdiction to reduce incarcerative sentence and substitute supervised release with a condition of home detention for the remaining sentence, after considering 18 U.S.C. § 3553(a) factors. Provides right to counsel appointed. [Author Note: This is not a compassionate release provision, but rather, a forced Pilot Program provision.]

2. Makes Covid-19 an automatic *extraordinary and compelling reason for compassionate release* for anyone who qualifies as 'high risk' under CDC guidelines, e.g. those over 60 years of age or younger

with underlying severe medical conditions. [Author Note: The First Step Act of 2018 already provides for judicial review of inmate filed motions for compassionate release denied at the BOP level, after exhaustion of administrative remedies; that also require a judicial review of 18 U.S.C. § 3553(a) factors, and other considerations by the court, prior to granting compassionate release.]

S. 1014 First Step Implementation Act 2021-

s. 1014 was introduced by Senator Richard J. Durbin (D-IL) in March, 2021. S. 1014 if passed would have a major impact, with retroactive application, for effected offense types.

There are some major changes in the works for drug offense sentencing, with retroactive application.

Interestingly, S. 1014 would create an array of new issues of first impression for United States District Courts to weigh through.

The substantive code amendments proposed in S. 1012 relate to:

1.) Controlled substances act, 21 U.S.C. §841 ("by striking "felony drug offense" and inserting "serious drug felony or serious violent felony", reducing the overall class of inmates that qualify for aggravated sentences) - with retroactive sentence reduction provisions and providing standing for inmates to file for reductions directly;

2.) Modifying safety valve provisions for drug offenses (including 'written waivers' of 18 U.S.C. 3553(f)(1) by the court); and

3.) Juvenile Parole, Sealing and Expungement provisions.

All things being equal, there should be some major changes, additions and supplements to the First Step Act passed in the 2021-2022 117th Congress, as bipartisan legislation.

The Authors opine that the most important of all changes proposed should include an inmate's right to complain directly to a District Court Judge following exhaustion of administrative remedies. That is needed in order to permit lawful redress by inmates, related to any underlying disparity or failure regarding any substantive right conferred by the First Step Act.

Critical Thinking-

The Authors intend for this publication to be a detailed review and analysis of multiple issues of first impression, relative to recidivism reduction programs and productive activities, in order to foster critical thinking regarding those topics and issues presented.

As always, Federal Sentencing Alliance invites constructive criticism, *peer review*, comment, or alternative argument, from the public, Congress, the Department of Justice, the Bureau of Prisons, or anyone else, regarding any matters presented in this publication. If you believe that our studied logic is flawed, please feel free to tell us why.

About Author Federal Sentencing Alliance-

Federal Sentencing Alliance headquartered in Florida, is a national consortium of federal sentencing mitigation specialists, federal sentencing legal writers, and supervisory members, that works directly with individual attorneys and law firms based in the United States for all federal sentencing assignments. Federal Sentencing Alliance is not a law firm, but rather, the sentencing mitigation expert that law firms hire.

This book was written for informational and educational purposes, and to inspire critical thinking regarding the issues presented, that will likely be the subject of debate by legal scholars for quite some time.

Federal Sentencing Alliance has Authored numerous First Step Act Of 2018 publications available on Amazon, including a low cost version of the current 2018 Federal Sentencing Guidelines from the United States Sentencing Commission, that will remain currently in effect until at least through November 1, 2022.

Federal Sentencing Alliance not a law firm and cannot give legal advice. Any such interpretation from this publication is completely unintended. You are encouraged, however, to seek legal advice regarding the matters presented in this publication, and to be guided by the sound advice of your attorney.

Joe Pappacoda, J.D., Nova Southeastern University, Davie, Florida, and B.S.B.A., Bryant University, Smithfield, Rhode Island, is the founding member of Federal Sentencing Alliance, and is the primary Author of most Federal Sentencing Alliance publications, available on Amazon and Barnes & Noble.

Joe is a <u>former</u> attorney, <u>former</u> forensic accountant, <u>former</u> state prosecutor, and <u>former</u> state special agent. Joe was directly involved in hundreds of criminal investigations, prosecutions, and defense cases, in one capacity or another, from 1991 through 2018, both civil and criminal, and in both state and federal courts.

Federal Sentencing Alliance may be contacted by email at: FederalSentencingAllinace@aol.com, or through the www.FederalSentencingAlliance.com contact Form on the Website.

About Author Ralph S. Behr-

Attorney Ralph S. Behr is the general counsel for Federal Sentencing Alliance, and has been an active Board Member for several years now.

Attorney Ralph S. Behr is also a practicing attorney admitted in Florida, New York, Oregon, United States District Courts in New York, Florida, Pennsylvania and the United States Supreme Court.

Attorney Behr is actively litigating matters of first impression in Federal Court(s) involving Sentencing Mitigation litigation under the First Step Act Of 2018, and is also on the Board Of Directors for Federal Sentencing Alliance.

Ralph is the Co-Chair of the Criminal Law Committee of the South Palm Beach County Bar

Association, former Chair of the Legislative Committee of the Democratic Party of Palm Beach County. Ralph is politically active in Judicial races in Florida and active in the World Justice Project, Washington, D.C., promoting the Rule of Law internationally since 2014.

Attorney Behr is a former Legislative Aide in the New York State Assembly, served multiple members of the New York State Penal Committee, a former Research and Legal Writing teaching assistant at Hofstra University School of Law, and a former Research Assistant for select projects at Thompson Reuters legal publications.

Ralph has achieved these awards and national recognitions:

- o A/V Rated by Martindale Hubbell in Criminal Trial Law

- America's Top 100 Criminal Lawyers in Florida 2020
- AVVO's highest rating of 10 out of 10
- Best Lawyers in America since 2006
- Board Certified in Criminal Trial Law by the Florida Bar since 2004
- Death Certified for Capital Murder Trial by the Florida Bar
- Florida's Super Lawyers since 2007
- National Super Lawyers
- Who's Who in American Law since 2007

Attorney Behr is available by calling (561) 717-3000, or by emailing: rb@lawbehr.com

Special Thanks to Joe Pappacoda, Federal Sentencing Alliance, for his intuition, insight, contributions, and tireless research.

© 2021 Federal Sentencing Alliance
© 2021 Ralph S. Behr

[All Rights Reserved]